GOD GUIDED
PURPOSES

GOD GUIDED
PURPOSES

THE JOURNEY INTO FULFILLING YOUR PURPOSE

ERIC C. BINGHAM, DMIN

Xulon Press

Xulon Press
2301 Lucien Way #415
Maitland, FL 32751
407.339.4217
www.xulonpress.com

© 2022 by Eric C. Bingham

All rights reserved solely by the author. The author guarantees all contents are original and do not infringe upon the legal rights of any other person or work. No part of this book may be reproduced in any form without the permission of the author.

Due to the changing nature of the Internet, if there are any web addresses, links, or URLs included in this manuscript, these may have been altered and may no longer be accessible. The views and opinions shared in this book belong solely to the author and do not necessarily reflect those of the publisher. The publisher therefore disclaims responsibility for the views or opinions expressed within the work.

Unless otherwise indicated, Scripture quotations taken from the English Standard Version (ESV). Copyright © 2001 by Crossway, a publishing ministry of Good News Publishers. Used by permission. All rights reserved.

Paperback ISBN-13: 978-1-66286-816-0
Ebook ISBN-13: 978-1-66286-817-7

ABSTRACT
God Guided Purposes: The Journey Into Fulfilling Your Purpose

Eric Courtland Bingham, M.Div., DMin

Keywords: Purpose, Followers, Acts 6, Influence, Widows, Priorities, Unity, Wisdom, adding to the Word of God, Biblically-based Solutions, Leadership, Spiritual Gifts, the will of God, Pleasing God, Excellence, Examples, Faith, Grace, Favor, Apologetics, Acts 7, Witness, Contrasting Response, Persecution, Acts 8, Witnessing, Teaching, Preaching, Christ, Glory of God, Deferment, Ministry, Understanding, Ministerial Opportunities, Acts 21, Evangelism, Prophecy, and Transformation.

The God ordained plan for the life of a follower of Jesus Christ is not the fulfillment of one singular purpose, but the fulfillment of the purposes that present themselves at any given time along the Christian journey. Jesus did not save us from sin simply to be saved from sin, but Jesus saved us so that we might live a life of righteousness through the fulfillment of the purposes that have been pre-ordained for His children. The purpose of this writing project is to provide an amalgamation of the purposes fulfilled throughout the life of Philip, who became known as "the evangelist," to provide a sense of the purposes to be fulfilled in the life of those who proclaim to have surrendered their lives to Christ.

Acknowledments

The first acknowledgement must and should always go to my Lord and Savior Jesus Christ who delivered me from darkness and put me on the righteous path which is found in His marvelous light.

The second acknowledgement goes to Trinity Seminary and Bible College which God used to enhance my Biblical knowledge and understanding culminating in this writing project.

The third acknowledgment goes to my lovely wife, Sharon Regina Bingham, who encouraged me, motivated me, and prayed for me during my educational journey.

And last but not least my wonderful mother, Dr. Bobbie A. Henderson, who offered very helpful writing suggestions during the writing process to help balance doctoral level authorship while maintaining understandability for a broader audience.

Table of Contents

Introduction	The Guide into Our Purpose	xi
Chapter One	Fulfilling God's Societal Purposes	1
Chapter Two	Fulfilling God's Influential Purposes	12
Chapter Three	Fulfilling God's Pleasure Purposes	26
Chapter Four	Fulfilling God's Exemplary Purposes	40
Chapter Five	Fulfilling God's Responsive Purposes	51
Chapter Six	Fulfilling God's Contrasting Purposes	61
Chapter Seven	Fulfilling God's Scatteration Purposes	71
Chapter Eight	Fulfilling God's Distinctive Purposes	80
Chapter Nine	Fulfilling God's Juxtapositional Purposes	88
Chapter Ten	Fulfilling God's Deferential Purposes	97
Chapter Eleven	Fulfilling God's Transitional Purposes	108
Chapter Twelve	Fulfilling God's Opportunistic Purposes	117
Chapter Thirteen	Fulfilling God's Transformative Purposes	131
Conclusion	Chapter Summarizations	141

INTRODUCTION
THE GUIDE INTO OUR PURPOSE

The believer's journey into their purpose begins with more than just believing in Jesus Christ. The journey of believers begins when they completely make up their minds to become avid followers of Christ. The calling on the life of the Apostles as revealed to us in Scripture was to do more than just believe in Christ; the first call upon their lives was to follow Him (e.g., Matthew 4:18-19). Christ's purpose in their lives to make them fishers of men would not be accomplished until they obeyed the command to follow Him. The Bible says that even the demons believe and tremble (James 2:19), but this type of belief most assuredly does not demonstrate that they themselves are followers of Christ. The type of belief that the demons possess is only an acknowledgement of who Christ is and the authority that He has over them (Mark 5:1-13), but what they do not possess is a desire to live a completely surrendered life to Him. From Mark 5:1-13, we see that the demons even bow down before Jesus, but to simply obey what He has commanded is considered torment to them and they would rather have Jesus fulfill their request as opposed to simply obeying what He would have them to do. The true believer in Jesus Christ must have a wholehearted desire to follow Him.

F. Scott Spencer describes the call to follow Jesus a call of imperativeness.[1] He insists that Jesus' call, specifically as it related to Peter, Andrew, James, John, and Matthew, was a call of liberation.[2] A call that set them free from the oppressive political system that they found themselves embedded. Spencer parallels the first disciples' liberation to the demoniac who was delivered from the "legion" of demons which he considers to be symbolic of the Roman soldiers of that era.[3] So, it is for all who heed the imperative call to follow Jesus Christ. Following Him is deliverance from this oppressive and sinful world in which we live, to live the translated and transformed life that God has designed for us to live (Colossians 1:13, Romans 12:2). He whom the Son sets free is free indeed (John 8:36).

To heed the call to follow Jesus Christ also delivers us from the way that seems right. Proverbs 14:11-12 intimates that the way that seems right only leads to the way of both destruction and death, but when we choose the way of the upright, we are delivered from death and destruction to the way that causes us to flourish. That way is by following Jesus Christ (John 14:6).

There are primarily five Synoptic events that provide insight into what it means to be a follower of Jesus Christ.[4] The first is the call of Simon (called Peter), Andrew, James, and John to follow Him so that He might make them fishers of men. Their response was to immediately leave behind their fishing business for the sake of following Jesus (Matthew 4:18-20, Mark 1:16-20). The second is the call of Matthew (aka Levi the son of Alpheus) to follow Him. Matthew's response was immediate as well, leaving behind what is historically described as a

---

[1] F. Scott Spencer, "'Follow Me: The Imperious Call of Jesus in the Synoptic Gospels," *Interpretation* 59, no. 2 (April 2005): 142-153, accessed October 24, 2019, ATLA Religion Database with ATLASerials, EBSCOhost.

[2] Ibid. 145.

[3] Spencer, 146.

[4] Ibid., 142.

hated but lucrative tax collecting business (Matthew 9:9, Mark 2:13-14, Luke 5:27-28).[5]

The third provides the revelation that following Jesus may mean leaving behind worldly comforts and making life's top priority the preaching of the kingdom of God (Matthew 8:18-22; Luke 9:57-62). The fourth emphasizes a life of self-denial and a willingness to endure whatever sufferings are associated with the life of following Christ (Matthew 16:24-26, Mark 8:34-37, Luke 9:23-25). The last describes caring more about having the treasures of heaven than personally possessing the riches of this world (Matthew 19:16-30, Mark 10:17-31, Luke 18:18-30). The commonality that exists in all five Synoptic events is a willingness to potentially exchange a lucrative, luxurious lifestyle for one that prioritizes God's will above everything else.

D. Edmond Hiebert informs us that the first disciples were not following Jesus blindly, they were following Him because they were keenly conscious of the unique nature of the One enlisting them as His followers.[6] They believed Jesus of Nazareth, the son of Joseph to be the coming Messiah, the Son of God, and the King of Israel (John 1:35-49) and it was the miracle of water being turned into wine that legitimized their belief (John 2:1-11). So, it should also be with everyone who has decided to follow Jesus. We should be convinced that He is the anointed one of whom it was prophesied should come (Luke 4:14-21). This is what is truly meant when we proclaim Jesus to be the Christ.

Following Jesus means that He is the role model for how we should live in this life. Hiebert expresses that Christ Himself must be the motivator of our Christian conduct.[7] One of the most beloved Scriptures in all the Bible dictates that all things will work together for the good of them that love God and are called according to His purpose (Romans

---

[5] Joseph Jacobs and Isaac Broyde, "Tax-Gatherers," JewishEncyclopedia.com, http://www.jewishencyclopedia.com/articles/14273-tax-gatherers.

[6] D. Edmond Hiebert, "Following Jesus," *Direction* 10, no. 2 (April 1981): 33, accessed October 28, 2019, ATLA Religion Database with ATLASerials, EBSCOhost.

[7] Ibid., 34.

8:28), but this truth is only applicable to those who have surrendered to what God has predestined and that is allowing Jesus to be the role model for their lives (Romans 8:29). After Jesus washed the disciples' feet, He explained to them that as their Lord and Teacher what He had just done was an example that He was setting for them to do also and if they wanted to be blessed then they must follow His example (John 13:1-17). As followers of Jesus Christ, if we want to be blessed then we must be imitators of the examples that He has set for us.

Charles F. Stanley reminds us that those who are followers of Jesus Christ are those who are considered to be born again.[8] Stanley provides nine characteristics which he believes are essential in the lives of those who are following Jesus, but as it relates to the fulfillment of our purpose, the one that seems the most crucial is the willingness to listen to Christ with the intent of obeying Him.[9]

After Jesus was transfigured before Peter, James, and John, they heard a voice from the cloud that covered them which said to them this is my beloved Son, with whom I am well pleased, listen to Him (Matthew 17:1-5). In almost "drop the mike" fashion, God says that the priority is listening to His beloved Son, Jesus Christ. For those of us who desire to fulfill the purpose to which we have been called, the characteristic of being a listener of Christ is crucial because it is through His Spirit that Christ speaks to us.

The Gospel of John shares with us that the Holy Spirit, aka our Advocate and the Spirit of truth who abides in us, teaches us and reminds us of the word that God has spoken to us. In particular, those who love Christ and have a zealousness for keeping His word (John 14:15-26). J. Lanier Burns states that obedience is an expression of love in the family of God and the Father rewards this love by manifesting

---

[8] Charles F. Stanley, "9 Characteristics of a Follower of Jesus: Committing Ourselves to Christ," In Touch Ministries, March 26, 2018, https://www.intouch.org/Read/Blog/9-characteristics-of-a-follower-of-jesus.

[9] Ibid.

Himself to those who are obedient.[10] The Holy Spirit does not provide the "reminders" of what Christ has said to those who do not have a zealousness to obey what He has said. This explains why the word of God does not seem to be a prevalent part of the lives of those who proclaim to be believers in Christ because their ultimate goal is not to obey Him.

The journey into purpose begins with the believer's heartfelt desire to love and obey the commandments of God; that same type of loving desire that David expressed in the Psalms (e.g., Psalm 119). That's why David cried out to God when he violated the commandments of God because he understood that sin disrupted his ability to hear from God. When David asked God to create in him a clean heart and renew a right spirit within him, David was asking God to restore his ability to communicate with Him (Psalm 51:10). It is through our spirit that we are able to communicate with God. Harry P. Nasuti insists that sin is the disruption of our relationship with God.[11] If God did not cleanse David's heart, then hearing from God would be difficult. For the believer in Jesus Christ, obedience to the word of God is imperative to hearing the voice of God because He only clearly speaks to the obedient.

Nasuti also defines sin as that which causes us to deviate from one's proper goal in life.[12] If our proper goal in life is to please God (2 Corinthians 5:9), then just like David we need to cry out to God to cleanse and renew us so that all hindrances to hearing His voice might be removed.

Within the pericope of John 14:15-25 (which describes the enhanced relationship that the followers of Christ have with His Spirit), John emphasizes that before we can be reminded of the word that God has

---

[10] J. Lanier Burns, "John 14:1-27: The Comfort of God's Presence," *Bibliotheca sacra* 172, no. 687 (Jul – Sep 2015): 311, accessed August 17, 2020, ATLA Religion Database with ATLASerials, EBSCOhost.

[11] Harry P. Nasuti, "Repentance and Transformation: The Role of the Spirit in Psalm 51," *The Bible Today* 57, no. 4 (Jul-Aug 2019): 215, accessed March 23, 2020, ATLA Religion Database with ATLASerials, EBSCOhost.

[12] Nasuti, 145.

spoken to us, then we need to be taught. We cannot be reminded of what God has said to us until we have been taught what God has said to us. If we are going to be able to hear God's Spirit when He speaks, then being taught is not optional, it is mandatory. God's desire for His people is to profit from the teaching of God's word because it equips us to fulfill the purposes to which He has called us (2 Timothy 3:16-17).

Patrick Nullens directs us to the admonishment given to Timothy to hold on to sound teaching with the faith and love that is in Christ Jesus. With the help of the Holy Spirit, Timothy was told to guard sound teaching as he would a treasure (2 Timothy 1:13-14).[13] The Holy Spirit considers sound teaching so important that He is willing to use His power to help us to guard it and hold on to it. Sound teaching is the treasured resource that the Holy Spirit draws from when He deems it necessary to bring it to our remembrance.

The Spirit that abides within the followers of Jesus Christ has empowered some with the gift to teach (Ephesians 4:11-12). God has provided some with the gift of teaching so that we might be taught. 1 Corinthians 12:28 hints to the essentialness of the gift of teaching and ranks it above miracles and the gift of healing. This may be blasphemous talk to some, but the gift of teaching and the gift of being taught (because teaching is a reciprocal process) according to the Scriptures outranks miracles and the gift of healing. Bert E. Downs points out that among the scholarly community the gift of teaching is considered one of God's major gifts because it is more than just the provision of someone's individual thoughts; it is the exposition of the words that have come from God Himself.[14] The teaching gift and the teacher who has

---

[13.] Patrick Nullens, "Theologia caritatis and the Moral Authority of Scripture: Approaching 2 Timothy 3:16-17 with a hermeneutic of love," *European Journal of Theology* 22, no. 1 (2013): 45, accessed March 24, 2020, ATLA Religion Database with ATLASerials, EBSCOhost.

[14.] Bert E. Downs, "The Spiritual Gift of Teaching," *Christian Education Journal* 6, no. 1 (1985): 63, accessed March 24, 2020, ATLA Religion Database with ATLASerials, EBSCOhost.

The Guide into Our Purpose

it are critical elements in the building up of the church.[15] It is through this perfecting and edifying work that we learn to recognize God's voice.

The parable supplied in John 10:1-6 contends that those who are followers of Jesus Christ know His voice. The teaching of the word of God familiarizes us with the voice of Jesus Christ and the Spirit through which He speaks. Familiarity with God's voice protects us from the voice of strangers who would have us follow their voice as opposed to following Christ. Those who are not being equipped through the teaching of the word of God place themselves in danger because they do not know the difference between God's voice and the deceptions of the ungodly. Callie Joubert and Nick Maartens stress the believer's responsibility to weigh carefully all things that appear to be a "word from the Lord."[16] The only legitimate resource that we possess that protects us from all things that appear to be a "word from the Lord" is the actual word that has been given to us by Lord. The only thing that can guard us from the deceptions of the ungodly is an intimate familiarity with the voice of God and therefore we need to be taught.

One of Luke's recollections was the nobility of the Jews who resided in Berea. What attributed to their nobility was the eagerness with which they received the word and their diligent practice of examining the Scriptures to assure that what was being said to them aligned with the Scriptures. This practice led to the belief of many (Acts 17:10-12). Our beliefs should not be solely based on what is said to us, but on how what is said to us aligns with the word of God. C.H. Elijah Sadaphal refers to such encounters as a connectivity between the Divine and humanity.[17] Our personal familiarity with the word of God that comes from being

---

[15] Ibid.

[16] Callie Joubert and Nick Maartens, "Hearing God's Voice: Evaluating Some Popular Teachings on the Subject," *Conspectus* 25, (25 March 2018): 52, accessed March 25, 2020, ATLA Religion Database with ATLASerials, EBSCOhost.

[17] C. H. Sadaphal, "Connectivity: Acts 17," *The Living Pulpit (Online)* 24, no. 4 (Winter 2015): 14-16, accessed March 26, 2020, ATLA Religion Database with ATLASerials, EBSCOhost.

God Guided Purposes

taught the word of God not only guards us from deception, but it can also deepen our beliefs and connect us to the One who is Divine.

The follower of Jesus Christ should guard him or herself from self-deception as well. Hebrews 4:11-12 teaches us that the word of God can keep us from falling into patterns of disobedience because it discerns the thoughts and intentions of each individual heart. Familiarity with the word of God aids us in determining whether the voice that I am hearing is actually from God or is it my own. Is it my own fears and perceptions that are speaking to me or is it actually God who is speaking to me? Jeremiah 17:9 provides the illumination that the heart is deceitful above all things and is desperately wicked. The word of God helps us to do battle against the thoughts and intents of my own deceitful and wicked heart. Since it is God's will that we succeed in fulfilling the purposes that He has called us to, He has provided His word to assure that the voice that we are hearing is indeed His.

Gene R. Smillie presses us to examine Hebrews 4:11-12 within its context (Hebrews 3:7-4:13).[18] Its context alludes to the forty-year rebellion of the Israelites in the wilderness; a rebellion against the word of God which resulted in a generation's failure to receive the promise of God. Smillie believes the theme of the context to be a division between those who believed the word of God from those who did not believe.[19] The context also reveals that the word of God can provide the revelation of what is in someone's heart, beliefs that align with the word of God and those which are contrary. We should allow the teaching of the word of God to dispel any beliefs which are contrary to God's word so that we will more clearly be able to detect His voice.

As believers in Jesus Christ who have committed ourselves to be followers of Jesus Christ, we should allow ourselves to be consistently baptized in the word that has come from God. Baptism in the word

---

[18] Gene R. Smillie, "'Ο λογοος του θεου' in Hebrews 4:12-13," *Novum Testamentum* 46, no. 4 (2004): 338-359, accessed March 28, 2020, ATLA Religion Database with ATLASerials, EBSCOhost.

[19] Ibid., 341.

of God is what familiarizes us with the voice of God so that when He speaks to us through His Spirit, we can be confident that it is Him who is speaking to us. Once we are confident that it is God who is speaking to us, then we must allow ourselves to be guided and led by what God has said through the reminders that are given to us by His Spirit.

The pinnacle of fulfilling the purposes of God is that God is glorified. It glorifies God when we are guided and led by what He has said. Jesus Christ ascended into heaven to be our Advocate with the Father (1 John 2:1). Jesus' ascension allowed Him to send His Spirit to be the Advocate who is with us (John 14:26, John 16:7). When the Spirit speaks to us, He is guiding us through the truths that have been declared to Him, the truths that glorify Christ (John 16:13-14). This can also be associated with the Divine connectivity spoken of by Sadaphal.[20] As those who are committed followers of Jesus Christ, we in turn glorify God when we are guided and led by those things that have been said to us by God (1 Corinthians 10:31). This becomes our witness to the world that we are truly the children of God (Romans 8:14), those who are working hard to fulfill the purposes of God.

Matt Searles indicates that the discourse in John 14 is bracketed by the phrase "Let not your hearts be troubled."[21] The comfort that the Holy Spirit was going to provide the disciples of Christ was to help alleviate any trouble that might burden their hearts. Though Christ would be absent from them, His Spirit would be with them to provide continual access to God and revelations from God.[22] As those who are consistently being baptized in the word of God, this makes us disciples of Jesus Christ as well. That same comfort that is provided from the Comforter is also available to us, especially those who allow themselves

---

[20] Sadaphal, 14-16.

[21] Matt Searles, "These Things I Have Said to You: An Investigation of How Purpose Clauses Govern the Interpretation of John 14-16," *Journal of the Evangelical Theological Society* 60, no. 3, (Sep 2017): 515-516, accessed March 29, 2020, ATLA Religion Database with ATLASerials, EBSCOhost.

[22] Ibid.

to be guided and led by the Spirit that was sent by Jesus Christ. This same Spirit is the Spirit which guides us into our purpose.

The purpose of this writing project is to examine the life of Philip, who eventually became to be known as "the Evangelist." Philip exemplifies a surrendered life to the guidance and leadership of the Holy Spirit (Acts 6-8, 21). The underlying goal of this writing project is to also maintain a level of simplicity. The theological community has a tendency of providing works which tend to go over the heads of the average Christian. With the Lord's help and His will, this writing project will seek to maintain a vernacular that reaches the largest audience possible while also providing edification to build them up. The hope of examining the life of Philip is to give us a sense of how the Spirit of God guides us into the purposes that God Himself has already preordained for us.

CHAPTER ONE
FULFILLING GOD'S SOCIETAL PURPOSES

Colossians 1:13-20 (ESV)

[13] He has delivered us from the domain of darkness and transferred us to the kingdom of His beloved Son, [14] in Whom we have redemption, the forgiveness of sins [15] He is the image of the invisible God, the firstborn of all creation. [16] For by Him all things were created, in heaven and on earth, visible and invisible, whether thrones or dominions or rulers or authorities—all things were created through Him and for Him. [17] And He is before all things, and in Him all things hold together. [18] And He is the head of the body, the church. He is the beginning, the firstborn from the dead, that in everything He might be preeminent. [19] For in Him all the fullness of God was pleased to dwell, [20] and through Him to reconcile to Himself all things, whether on earth or in heaven, making peace by the blood of His cross.

Before we can fulfill any individualistic purposes that God may have for our lives, we need to fulfill the societal purposes that God has planned for us. Prior to God revealing the individual purposes that He had for Philip's life, God revealed the societal influences and purposes that both impacted and needed to be fulfilled in Philip's life. As followers of Jesus Christ who seek to fulfill the purposes of God, there are societal influences and purposes that need to be fulfilled in our own lives as well. Jason Lanker stresses that it is within the family of faith that strong relationships with others can significantly influence one's level of spiritual development.[23]

When the second person of the Trinity humbled Himself and took on human form (John 1:1,14, Philippians 2:5-8), He came down from heaven (John 6:38) on a rescue mission (Luke 19:10). That rescue mission was to deliver us from the domain of darkness. The author Luke tells us that the domain of darkness from which Jesus came to deliver us from was the power of Satan (Acts 26:18). Norman L. Geisler refers to the dominion through which Satan exercises His power as the rebel kingdom,[24] the kingdom of those who reject the light of the knowledge of the glory of God which has been given to us in the face of Jesus Christ (2 Corinthians 4:6).

The followers of Jesus Christ have a societal connection to one another through the common testimony that we have with one another. We all have been delivered from the power of Satan. Wherever there are societal connections, there will also be societal influences and purposes that need to be fulfilled and so it is with those who have the testimony of being delivered from Satan's influence and placed under the sovereignty of the rightful King.[25]

Deliverance from something also means deliverance to something. The followers of Jesus Christ have been transferred into the kingdom of His beloved Son. The term kingdom infers that there is a king. Without

---

[23.] Jason Lanker, "The Family of Faith: The Place of Natural Mentoring in the Church's Christian Formation of Adolescents," *Christian Education Journal* 7, no. 2 (Fall 2010): 268, accessed August 25, 2020, ATLA Religion Database with ATLASerials, EBSCOhost.

[24.] Norman L. Geisler, *Bible Knowledge Commentary: An Exposition of the Scriptures by Dallas Seminary Faculty: New Testament Edition*, ed. John F. Walvoord and Roy B. Zuck (Colorado Springs: Chariot Victor Publishing, 1983), 672.

[25.] Ibid.

a king there can be no kingdom. Our King is God's beloved Son, Jesus Christ. The very first societal purpose that should be fulfilled in the lives of the followers of Jesus Christ should be our undaunting allegiance to Jesus Christ as King. Matthew W. Bates insists that an allegiance to Jesus Christ as King means more than just professing that Jesus is Lord, it also means being completely loyal to Christ and having a willingness to share the high point of the good news that Jesus is the enthroned King.[26]

One of the greatest Biblical demonstrations of an allegiance to Jesus Christ as King is found in Acts 5:12-42. This pericope, in short, describes the apostle's imprisonment and their angelic deliverance that they might continue to teach "all the words of this Life." Matthew Poole reminds us of the previous restrictions that had been placed on the disciples as witnesses (Matthew 16:20, Matthew 17:9), but the words spoken to them at the time of their deliverance lifted all restrictions.[27] They were to teach "all the words of this Life."

When the high priest and his associates became aware of the apostle's miraculous deliverance, they sent officers to detain them for a second time. The council of the high priest and his associates reminded the apostles of the charge against them; the charge that they were no to longer teach in the name of Lord. An additional emphasis that Luke delineates in this pericope is that the success of the church was not ultimately due to the signs and wonders that were being performed by the apostles (Acts 5:12). The Pulpit Commentary expresses that the signs and wonders performed by the apostles were intended to be a demonstration of the truth of Christianity.[28] The success of the church was due to what the apostles were teaching (Acts 5:28, 42). They were teaching in the name of the Lord.

---

[26]. Matthew W. Bates, Salvation by Allegiance Alone: Rethinking Faith, Works, and the Gospel of Jesus the King (Grand Rapids: Baker Academic, 2017), chap. 9, Kindle.

[27]. Matthew Poole, "Matthew Poole's Commentary," Bible Hub, accessed April 15, 2020, https://biblehub.com/commentaries/poole/acts/5.htm.

[28]. "Pulpit Commentary," Bible Hub, accessed August 19, 2020, https://biblehub.com/commentaries/pulpit/acts/2.htm.

The apostle's reply to the reiterated charges was that they must obey God rather than men and continue to witness to the fact that Jesus is the exalted Leader and Savior who sits at the right hand of the throne of God. Kylie Crabbe points out that in the course of the narrative the apostles' obedience was to the divine agent that was sent to set them free from the prison.[29] In like fashion, everyone who declares themselves to be followers of Jesus Christ should take advantage of every opportunity to declare and demonstrate their allegiance to Jesus as the enthroned King since He is the one who set us free from our prison, the domain of darkness.

The phrase beloved Son is an echo of Jesus' baptism (Matthew 3:17, et al.) and the event that occurred on the Mount of Transfiguration (Matthew 17:5, *et al.*). In both instances, the voice of God is heard declaring that Jesus is God's beloved Son, in whom He is well pleased. The second instance includes the commandment to listen to Jesus. If context should tell us anything, then water baptism and listening to the words of Christ are both pleasing to God. Since our aim is to please God (2 Corinthians 5:9), then water baptism (which Jesus calls a fulfillment of righteousness, Matthew 3:15) and listening to the words of Christ should be high on our list of priorities.

John Behr insightfully provides that the connection of the "kingdom" with the "Son" is the fulfillment of the promise that was made to David (2 Samuel 7:12-14).[30] Bates insists that the metaphorical language found in 2 Samuel 7:12-14 would have been recognized as an anticipation of a future reality: Jesus as the only begotten Son of God.[31] Jesus Christ is the forever King who sits on a forever throne and rules over a forever

---

[29] Kylie Crabbe, "Being Found Fighting Against God: Luke's Gamaliel and Josephus on Human Responses to Divine Providence," *Zeitschrift für die neutestamentliche Wissenschaft und die Kunde der älteren Kirche* 106, no. 1 (2015): 32, accessed April 18, 2020, ATLA Religion Database with ATLASerials, EBSCO host.

[30] John Behr, "Colossians 1:13-20: A Chiastic Reading," *St. Vladimir's Theological Quarterly* 40, no.4 (1996): 250, accessed April 14, 2020, ATLA Religion Database with ATLASerials, EBSCOhost.

[31] Bates, chap. 2, Kindle.

kingdom (Hebrews 1:8). The society that the followers of Jesus Christ have been transferred into is a society that will endure forever and so should be the allegiance that we have given to Christ Jesus as King. Our allegiance should be an allegiance that endures forever.

Scripture expresses that there is nothing that can separate us from the love of God in Christ Jesus our Lord (Romans 8:35-39). Kristofer Coffman tells us that this section of Scripture is sometimes identified as Paul's "Hymn to God's Love."[32] Our demonstrated sentiments toward Christ Jesus should express the same, sentiments that demonstrate that we have an allegiance with Jesus Christ from which we refuse to be separated.

Whenever Jesus Christ is referred to as His beloved Son it should remind us of the lengths that Jesus Christ went to that we might have a reserved place in His eternal kingdom (1 Peter 1:3-4). Bates summarizes Christ's efforts as the eight stages of Jesus' life story (the gospel). The summary includes how Christ preexisted with the Father [John 1:1, Philippians 2:6], how He took on human flesh [John 1:14, Philippians 2:7], how He died in accordance with the Scriptures [1 Corinthians 15:3], how He was buried, but how He was raised on the third day in accordance with the Scriptures [1 Corinthians 15:4], how He appeared to many [1 Corinthians 15:5-8], how He is currently seated at the right hand of God [Hebrews 1:3, et al.], and how He will come again as Judge [2 Timothy 4:1].[33] In sharing the gospel (Jesus' life story) with those who have yet to become followers of Jesus Christ, we have a societal responsibility to present the gospel with this same level of clarity so that unbelievers will be clear about the lengths that God went to so that they could have a place in His kingdom. Lanker calls the gospel

---

[32.] Kristofer Coffman, "Powers and Authorities: Preaching Romans 8:35-39," *Word & World* 39, no, 3 (Sum 2019): 275, accessed August 20, 2020, ATLA Religion Database with ATLASerials, EBSCOhost.

[33.] Bates, chap. 9, Kindle.

our inheritance.[34] It should be an inheritance that we are unashamed to share with those who have yet to believe (Romans 1:16).

A great extent of the world's biblical understanding of God's love begins and ends with John 3:16. It is the societal responsibility of those who are followers of Jesus Christ to provide clarification for what is meant by "God so loved the world that He gave His only begotten Son." Patrick S. Franklin details that it was human redemption that set God's love in motion and it is actualized in the life of believers through the power of the Holy Spirit.[35] Sharing the eight stages of Christ's life story (the clarified gospel) recommended by Bates adds the elucidation necessary to provide a better understanding of the "so love" of God. The apostle Paul prayed that all saints have this same comprehension of the knowledge of Christ's love (Ephesians 3:18-19) so that we might be better equipped to do the work of the church. Sharing the eight stages of Christ's life story assists in providing the comprehension prayed for by the apostle Paul.

Scripture synonymously refers to the kingdom of His beloved Son as the kingdom of God or the kingdom of heaven. Kaufmann Kohler expresses, that to the ancient Hebrews, "heaven" came to be used as an equivalent for "God" since the God of Israel is eminently the God of heaven. This is why we find the gospel of Matthew preserving the term "kingdom of heaven" where the other gospels have "kingdom of God."[36]

Jewish tradition describes acknowledging God as the only sovereign King as "taking the yoke of the kingdom of God." Taking the yoke of the kingdom of God also means taking the yoke of the Torah (i.e.,

---

[34] Lanker, 270.

[35] Patrick S. Franklin, "The God Who Sends is The God Who Loves: Mission as Participating in the Ecstatic Love of the Triune God," Didaskalia 28, (2017-2018): 75-76, accessed April 20, 2020, ATLA Religion Database with ATLASerials, EBSCOhost.

[36] Kaufmann Kohler, "Heaven," JewishEncyclopedia.com, accessed April 18, 2020, http://www.jewishencyclopedia.com/articles/7440-heaven.

the commandments of God).³⁷ Followers of Jesus Christ cannot fulfill their purpose unless they are willing to take on the yoke of the commandments of God and completely surrender their will to His (Matthew 6:10).

The kingdom of God is also identified as the kingdom of the Christ (Ephesians 5:5). In passages such as Matthew 3:2, Jesus announces that the kingdom of heaven is at hand. Jesus made this announcement because the kingdom of heaven's King had come near. When Pilate asked Jesus if He was the king of the Jews, Jesus answered you have said so (Luke 23:3). Jesus' acknowledgement that He indeed is King of the Jews is not meant to be exclusive, but is inclusive of everyone who acknowledges the truth of Jesus' kingship (John 18:37). S. Dean McBride, Jr. shares that it is only Christ alone who now offers "the yoke of the kingdom of Heaven."³⁸

The followers of Jesus Christ are referred to as having their citizenship in heaven (Philippians 3:20), contextually described as those who have set aside all worldly identifications, accomplishments, and goals to pursue the goal of having a more intimate relationship with Jesus Christ. For the followers of Jesus Christ, the associations of this world should be considered scraps compared to being associated with Jesus Christ as Lord, Savior, and King. The honor of being a citizen of heaven should be valued high and above any worldly identifications, accomplishments, or goals that we could ever possess or achieve. No matter how illustrious the lofty goals of this world seem to appear, none should rank close to having an intimate relationship with Jesus Christ (Philippians 3:8).

The original Greek word from which we have translated citizenship (preferred by most modern translations) is πολίτευμα (the

---

[37] Kaufmann Kohler, "Kingdom of God ("Malkuta de-Adonai")," JewishEncyclopedia.com, accessed April 18, 2020, http://www.jewishencyclopedia.com/articles/9328-kingdom-of-god.

[38] S. Dean McBride, "The Yoke of the Kingdom: An Exposition of Deuteronomy 6:4-5," *Interpretation* 27, no. 3 (Jul 1973): 285, accessed April 22, 2020, ATLA Religion Database with ATLASerials, EBSCOhost.

transliteration is *politeuma*).[39] Scholars such as Samuel Guy prefer the translation of commonwealth which is broadly described as a communal entity from which social or political identity is derived.[40] As citizens of the communal entity of the kingdom of heaven, we should derive both our social and political identities from it and should be unashamed to publicly identify ourselves as such (Luke 9:23-26). Jesus is our King, our societal community is the kingdom of heaven, and the redeemed of the Lord (those who have been delivered from the domain of darkness) should say so (Psalm 107:2).

Guy argues against the Roman culture being the dominant culture in Philippi for the dominance of Greek-speaking noncitizens.[41] It would seem that the recipients identified in the letter to the Philippians does not argue for or against either. The apostle Paul specifically identifies all the saints in Christ Jesus who are at Philippi as the target recipients of his letter (Philippians 1:1). Paul places no emphasis on any culture above another. If they were saints in Christ Jesus, then they were citizens of heaven. Among the followers of Jesus Christ, there should be no cultural emphasis identified among us. For in Christ Jesus, we are all sons of God through faith (Galatians 3:26). Doug Heidebrecht associates Galatians 3:26 with Ephesians 2:14 which describes how Christ has broken down in His flesh all divisions that may have existed among us.[42] The only cultural identity that should be of any significance should be if you are a saint in Christ Jesus and a citizen of the kingdom of heaven.

---

[39] W.E. Vine, *Vine's Expository Dictionary of Old & New Testament Words* (Nashville: Thomas Nelson Publishers, 1997), 185.

[40] Samuel Guy, "A Politeuma Worth Pursuing: Philippians 3:20 in Light of Philippi's Sociological Composition," *Stone-Campbell Journal* 22, no. 1 (Spr 2019): 90, 98, accessed April 23, 2020, ATLA Religion Database with ATLASerials, EBSCO host.

[41] Ibid., 89-100.

[42] Doug Heidebrecht, "Distinction and Function in the Church: Reading Galatians 3:38 in Context," *Direction* 34, no. 2 (Fall 2005): 185, accessed August 21, 2020, ATLA Religion Database with ATLASerials, EBSCO host.

The Greek root word from which πολίτευμα (*politeuma*) is derived is πολιτεύομαι (*politeuomai*).⁴³ Its emphasis is placed on the behavior of a citizen. As the apostle Paul stood before the Sanhedrin, he exclaimed that he had lived his life (*politeuomai*) before God in all good conscience up to that day (Acts 32:1). Fulfillment of our social purposes should go beyond social and political identifications, but it should also include how we live our lives before God (Proverbs 15:3). The followers of Jesus Christ should live their lives according to God's will because this is what honors and pleases Him (Colossians 1:10).

Returning to the focus pericope for this chapter, the apostle Paul synonymously associates the kingdom of God's Son with the church (vs. 18). Jesus Christ is identified as the head of the body and the body is identified as the church. The society that the followers of Jesus Christ are transferred into is also known as the body of Christ, the church. Too often we visualize the church as being a building, but the visualization that should come to mind is the society of the followers of Jesus Christ. As the society of the followers of Jesus Christ, we have been mandated to acknowledge the preeminence of Christ. The beloved Son of God (vs. 13) did the very thing that pleased God (vs. 19) by shedding His blood upon the cross giving us peace with God and providing us the opportunity to be reconciled to God (vs. 20). Without Christ, we would still be held captive in the domain of darkness (vs. 13) and therefore the followers of Jesus Christ should acknowledge Christ's preeminence in every aspect of their lives (vs. 18).

Grant Macaskill notes the association of Christ's preeminence and His moniker of being the firstborn (first born of every creature and first born from the dead).⁴⁴ Macaskill insists that the moniker of being the

---

[43.] James Strong, "A Concise Dictionary of the Words in The Greek Testament; with their Renderings in the Authorized English Version" in *The New Strong's Exhaustive Concordance of the Bible* (Nashville: Thomas Nelson Publishers, 1990), 59, G4175/G4176.

[44.] Grant Macaskill, "Union(s) with Christ: Colossians 1:15-20," *Ex auditu* 33, (2017): 98, accessed April 27, 2020, ATLA Religion Database with ATLASerials, EBSCO host.

first born emphasizes the shared nature of Christ to His human creations. Christ is able to sustain the created realm because of His own creatureliness and He is able to bring life to the dead because He shared in their mortality.[45] A more completed thought to Macaskill's observation is Christ's shared nature with God (vs. 19). Christ's own creatureliness would not have been enough to bring life to the dead, but it is also because He possess the fullness of God (Acts 2:24). This is also why Christ is identified as the beginning (vs. 18), which can be understood contextually as the beginning of the church because He is the first of many brethren who will be born from the dead (1 Corinthians 15:20-23). He is preeminent.

Thayer's Greek Lexicon defines the church as a gathering of citizens.[46] One of the overlooked Biblical synonyms for the followers of Jesus Christ as a society of people is that we are also known as a gathering (aka an assembly or a congregation). One of the things that pleases God is to see His people gathered together. Even though we are currently a scattered people throughout the nations, one day God is going to gather us all together again (2 Thessalonians 2:1).

Until that day, passages such as Hebrews 10:24-26 informs us of the societal purpose of gathering ourselves together so that we can stir up one another to love (obviously in the same way that Christ has loved us, John 13:34), to do good deeds (deeds that glorify God, Matthew 5:16) and be an encouragement to one another. Failure to meet the societal purposes associated with gathering ourselves together is defined as neglect and deliberate sin. God has called the followers of Jesus Christ to be a blessing to one another evident through the plethora of "one another" passages that exist in Scripture.

In summation, those who consider themselves to be followers of Jesus Christ have societal purposes that they have been mandated to fulfill. The mandated societal purposes begin with our undaunting

---

[45] Ibid., 99.

[46] "G1577 – ekklēsia–Thayer's Greek Lexicon," Blue Letter Bible, accessed April 28, 2020, https://www.blueletterbible.org/lang/lexicon/lexicon.cfm?Strongs=G1577&t=ESV.

allegiance to Jesus Christ as our King. This undaunting allegiance must be more than just through verbal identification; it must be demonstrated by how we live our lives through our obedience to all that God has commanded (John 14:15). Obedience to all that God has commanded exemplifies our loyalty to the kingdom of Christ as its citizens. The honor of being a citizen of the kingdom of Christ should be valued high and above any worldly identifications, accomplishments, or goals that we could ever possess or achieve.

Among the followers of Jesus Christ, there should be no cultural emphasis identified among us. The only cultural identity that should be of any significance should be if you are a saint in Christ Jesus and a citizen of the kingdom of heaven. To be effective witnesses for Jesus Christ, we have the societal responsibility to clearly understand every aspect of the gospel (the story of Christ) so that when the opportunity presents itself, we will be able to share and provide that understanding. As followers of Jesus Christ, we should never fail to gather ourselves together that we might stir up one another to love and do good deeds. This is also representative of Christ's desire to gather us all together upon His return. Through these things we fulfill the societal purpose of acknowledging the preeminence of Christ.

CHAPTER TWO
Fulfilling God's Influential Purposes

Acts 6:1-4 (ESV)

¹Now in these days when the disciples were increasing in number, a complaint by the Hellenists arose against the Hebrews because their widows were being neglected in the daily distribution. ² And the twelve summoned the full number of the disciples and said, "It is not right that we should give up preaching the word of God to serve tables. ³ Therefore, brothers, pick out from among you seven men of good repute, full of the Spirit and of wisdom, whom we will appoint to this duty. ⁴ But we will devote ourselves to prayer and to the ministry of the word."

Luke's introduction to the life of Philip (who would become known as the evangelist) begins by describing the positive influences that impacted his life. For those who have a yearning to fulfill the purposes of God in their lives, positive influences are vital to our development as followers of Jesus Christ. The Bible advises us that we should have people in our lives who will sharpen us (Proverbs 27:17) and those who will help us to become wise rather than those who might harm us (Proverbs 13:20). Bruce Waltke identifies these types of influences as true friendships.[47] The Bible also provides the admonishment that those who are living immoral lives will have a negative impact upon the lives of the followers of Jesus Christ especially those who are lacking in their knowledge of God (1 Corinthians 15:33-34). John W. Ritenbaugh provides that we tend to take on the character of the group with which we associate.[48] Therefore, it is incumbent upon us to be cautious about those with whom we allow to have an influence upon our lives.

One of the first influences upon the life of Philip was the community with which he was connected. Luke informs us that Philip was a member of a growing community of disciples. Luke's specific choice wasn't to tell us that this was a community of believers, but this community was a community of disciples.

In Acts 2:42-47, Luke described this community as believers who were devoted to the apostles' teaching and those who were intimately devoted to one another. Gary L. Carver relays that it was their commitment to each other in community which enabled them to be an uncommon, even extraordinary people.[49] It was this type of community through which God was not only performing many signs and wonders, but He was also adding to their number daily. This should speak volumes to the communities of believers (i.e., churches) who are concerned about their lack of effectiveness and growth. Failure to be committed to the teachings of the word of God and failure to be intimately devoted to one another as followers of Jesus Christ may be the very thing that stifles effectiveness and growth. The preference for the followers of Jesus Christ should be to flourish and not to be stifled.

[47.] Bruce Waltke, "Friends and Friendship in the Book of Proverbs: An Exposition of Proverbs 27:1-22," *Crux* 38, no. 3 (Sep 2002): 36, accessed August 10, 2020, ATLA Religion Database with ATLASerials, EBSCOhost.

[48.] John W. Ritenbaugh, "Commentaries: Forerunner Commentary – 1 Corinthians 15:33," BIBLETOOLS, accessed August 25, 2020, https://www.bibletools.org/index.cfm/fuseaction/bible.show/sVerseID/28752/eVerseID/28752.

[49.] Gary L. Carver, "Acts 2:42-47," *Review & Expositor* 87, no. 3 (Sum 1990): 476, accessed August 25, 2020, ATLA Religion Database with ATLASerials, EBSCOhost.

Craig S. Keener reminds us that this community of devotees was exhibiting a radical lifestyle change that had been impacted by the outpouring of God's Spirit. Those who valued people more than they did their possessions.[50] God wants His people to be connected and influenced by those who are being radically impacted by the presence of His Spirit. Since this is what God wants for His people, then this should also be what God's people should want for themselves.

W.E. Vine emphasizes that the Biblical definition of a disciple is one who is not only a pupil, but an adherent. This is why a disciple is spoken of as imitators of their teacher.[51] Matt Slick insists that to be a disciple of Christ means that you study His words, see what He did, and then do what He said and did.[52] Jesus Christ Himself said that those who are really His disciples are those who hold to His teaching (John 8:31). Our closest associations should be those who are more than just hearers of the word of God, but those whose truest intent is to obey those things that the word of God has commanded. James 1:22-25 dictates that this is the pathway to being blessed. We should be tightly connected to those who do more than just express a desire to be blessed but those who demonstrate that desire through their adherence to the word of God.

1 John 1 defines this community as the fellowship of those who have eternal life (1 John 1:2); those who are in fellowship with the Father and the Son, Jesus Christ (1 John 1:3). To receive the maximum benefits of this relationship, we must be devoted practitioners of the truth that has been revealed in the word of God (1 John 1:7, Deuteronomy 29:29). Our closest associations should be with those who are like-minded, those who are committed to maintaining their fellowship with God by

---

[50] Craig S. Keener, *The IVP Bible Background Commentary New Testament*, (Downers Grove: Intervarsity Press, 1993), 330.

[51] W. E. Vine, *Vine's Expository Dictionary of Old & New Testament Words*, (Nashville: Thomas Nelson Publishers, 1997), 308.

[52] Matt Slick, "Acts 6:1-7 Building the Church of Disciples," CARM: Christian Apologetics & Research Ministry, accessed August 25, 2020, https://carm.org/sermon-acts-6-1-7-building-church-disciples.

being obedient to the word that comes from God. These are the types of people that we should want to have an influence upon our lives.

Harald Hegstad furnishes the observation of the ambiguity that exists in the modern church. He labels this ambiguity the inner differentiation among church members.[53] Hegstad describes that there are those who exist in the church who might simply be called church folk, but there are also those who seem to make up a separate community within the church, the community of the faithful.[54] It is incumbent upon those who are seeking to fulfill the purposes of God to allow their strongest connections within the church to be with those who are within the community of the faithful. Even though our strongest connections should be with the community of the faithful, we should not disconnect ourselves from "church folk" in the hopes of drawing them into the community of the faithful as well.

Luke (author of the book of Acts) honestly provides that even among the community of disciples, problems can arise; problems that are a threat to the unity of the community of the faithful. Generically this conveys that situations and circumstances that arise among the community of the faithful are influential factors in our lives as well. Luke explains that this particular problem was a complaint by the Hellenists against the Hebrews because their widows were being neglected in the daily distribution.

Majority scholarly consensus describes the Hellenists as Jews whose dominant language was Greek and the Hebrews are described as Jews whose dominant language was Aramaic.[55] If the majority consensus is

---

[53.] Harald Hegstad, "A Minority Within the Majority: On the Relation Between the Church as Folk Church and as a Community of Believers," *Studia Theologica* 53, no. 2 (1999): 120, accessed April 6, 2020, ATLA Religion Database with ATLASerials, EBSCOhost.

[54.] Ibid., 121.

[55.] David W. Pao, "Waiters or Preachers: Acts 6:1-7 and the Lukan Table Fellowship Motif," *Journal of Biblical Literature* 130, no. 1 (2011): 127-128, accessed July 15, 2019, ATLA Religion Database with ATLASerials, EBSCOhost.

correct, this leads us to understand that the issue existed between those who were of the same ethnicity but possessed some cultural differences.

Unfortunately, scholarly consensus has not been reached over what is meant by the daily distribution. Most modern translations include that this was a daily distribution of food. Scholars such as John Gill believe that the daily distributions were more than just food, but also included monetary provisions.[56] Scholars who are of the same mindset as Pao believe that the daily distribution also included ministry of the word of God.[57]

Contextually it seems obvious that regardless of what is specifically meant by the daily distribution, Luke's focus seems to be centralized on the disruption that was threatening the unity of the community. Concern should be elevated within the followers of Jesus Christ when problems arise that threaten unity.

The Apostle Paul urged the faithful in Jesus Christ to have an eagerness to maintain the unity of the Spirit (Ephesians 4:3) because this eagerness exemplifies a lifestyle that is worthy of the divine calling of God (Ephesians 4:1). For those of us who are trying to fulfill the purposes of God, we should crave to live a lifestyle that is worthy of the divine calling of God and one of the ways that we do this is by attacking anything that threatens the unity within the community of the faithful.

God has called us all to be maintenance men. As maintenance men, we all bear the responsibility of maintaining the unity that we have as a community of disciples. James R. Payton, Jr. calls unity a necessary thing, which is why Christ so frequently prayed for unity.[58] Evil has the propensity to either abruptly or even silently raise its ugly head within our midst to try to disrupt the unity that exists among the

---

[56] John Gill, *Exposition of the Old and New Testament*, accessed July 12, 2019, http://www.sacred-texts.com/bib/cmt/gill/act006.htm.

[57] Pao, 127-144.

[58] James R. Payton, Jr., "On Unity and Truth: Martin Bucer's Sermon on John 17," *Calvin Theological Journal* 27, no. 1 (Apr 1992): 34, accessed August 27, 2020, ATLA Religion Database with ATLASerials, EBSCOhost.

faithful. It is the responsibility of the faithful to attack every threat that attempts to do so.

When Jesus Christ responded to Simon Peter's acknowledgment that He indeed was the Christ, the Son of the living God, Christ's response included that it was upon this rock that He would build His church and the gates of hell would not prevail against it (Matthew 16:15-19). Howard Horton provides that among the churches of Christ the understanding of Christ's response is just as it reads, the gates of Hades [hell] shall not prevent the building of the church.[59] The inference found in Christ's response to Peter was that the gates of hell would indeed take its shot at being a deterrent against what Christ is building up. Since Christ is still building His church, this means that hell is still taking its shot. One of the ways that the gates of hell take its shot is by attacking the church's unity, but the church (which includes those who have made the same confession and acknowledgment as Peter) has been given the keys to the kingdom (the revelations of God's word) to thwart hell's attacks so that we can maintain unity.

Isam E. Ballenger refers to our efforts to maintain unity as the mission and life of the church. We are called to be participants with God in removing any barriers to our connectedness with each other and with God. The community of disciples (a.k.a., the church) is supposed to be the exemplification of unity and harmony.[60] We should make every effort to maintain what God has ordained for us.

An interesting observation within the context of Ephesians 4 and its theme of unity is the mandate of the apostles to equip the saints for the work of ministry and the building up of the body of Christ. What makes this observation so interesting is how it connects to Acts 6:1-4 (the focus pericope for this chapter). The gift of the apostles and the gift

---

[59.] Howard Horton, "The Gates of Hades Shall Not Prevail Against It," *Restoration Quarterly* 5, no. 1 (1961): 4, accessed August 26, 2020, ATLA Religion Database with ATLASerials, EBSCOhost.

[60.] Isam E. Ballenger, "Ephesians 4:1-16," *Interpretation* 51, no. 3 (Jul 1997): 292-293, accessed April 7, 2020, ATLA Religion Database with ATLASerials, EBSCOhost.

within the apostles, according to Ephesians 4, should be focused upon equipping the saints for the work of maintaining and attaining unity within the community of the faithful. The twelve's (apostles) pursuit in Acts 6:1-4 appears to be doing just that.

Therefore, it is worth the effort of looking intently into how the twelve responded to the potential disruption that had arisen because these are the types of leaders who were an influence upon the life of Philip and these should also be the types of leaders that we should want as an influence in our lives as well.

Future leaders within the body of Christ should be drawn from the community of the faithful. Annette Huizenga points out that the faithful are those who are true heirs of the gospel truths that have been handed down.[61] If leadership within the body of Christ is God's purpose for us (which on some level we all are or will be whether it be at home, the workplace, and/or within the church), then being influenced by gifted and faithful leaders is beneficial to what God would have us to become.

In the focus pericope for this chapter, Luke does not mention one single apostle by name but only refers to them as a group. If the apostles were going to be successful in equipping the community of disciples for the work of maintaining unity, then they needed to demonstrate unity amongst themselves. They needed to be an example.

Scripture insists that the type of leaders whom we should allow to be influential in our lives should be those who are willing to be an example. The Apostle Peter admonishes elders to be an example for those who are in their charge (1 Peter 5:1-3). As one of those who was numbered with the twelve, Peter could rightly admonish the elders to be an example because he had already demonstrated himself to be willing to be an example himself. Albert Barnes describes this as the

---

[61.] Annette Bourland Huizenga, "Paul as Pastor in 1 Timothy, 2 Timothy, and Titus," *The Bible Today* 51, no. 5 (Sep-Oct 2013): 299, accessed August 27, 2020, ATLA Religion Database with ATLASerials, EBSCOhost.

appropriate character for a minister of the gospel.[62] Those who have an influence upon our lives should be those who are willing to be an example of those things which are being taught.

The problem that arose amongst the disciples in our focus pericope for this chapter is described as a complaint. The Outline of Biblical Usage defines the word complaint in this context as a murmuring, a secret debate, or a secret displeasure not openly avowed.[63] This justifies the King James version's depiction of the problem as being a murmuring. This may be evidential of the twelve's closeness to the community of disciples. Their nearness to those whom they served allowed them to become aware of the problem before it became an open dispute. The type of leaders that we should want to be an influence in our lives should be those who are close to the community of the faithful; close enough to be aware of problems that arise in their infancy and act quickly to put them to rest.

In his book, "Pastoral Leadership," Robert D. Dale describes what he defines as an encourager leader.[64] Dale uses Joseph who was also called Barnabas (Acts 4:36) as a model to expound upon the characteristics of an encourager leader. The characteristics include being a people-oriented leader, being generous with needy believers, able to manage conflict effectively, and being a trusted negotiator when looking for solutions to problems that exist within the body of Christ.[65] Interestingly enough, these same characteristics that were demonstrated by Barnabas can easily be identified as being demonstrated by the twelve as well. Since Barnabas spent his early Christian years under

---

[62.] Albert Barnes, "Commentary on 1 Peter 5:3," in *Barnes' Notes on the Whole Bible*, accessed May 20, 2020, https://www.studylight.org/commentaries/bnb/1-peter-5.html#3.

[63.] "G1112 – gongysmos–Outline of Biblical Usage," Blue Letter Bible, accessed May 20, 2020, https://www.blueletterBible.org/lang/lexicon/lexicon.cfm?Strongs=G1112&t=ESV.

[64.] Robert D. Dale, *Pastoral Leadership* (Nashville: Abingdon Press 1986), 71.

[65.] Ibid., 71-74.

the leadership of the twelve, it makes one wonder if it was the influence of the twelve that caused these same characteristics to be developed within Barnabas. If the follower of Jesus Christ wants to fulfill the influential purposes of God in his life, then caution should be taken to assure that those who are influential in our lives exhibit the same characteristics that God wants to see demonstrated in us (1 Corinthians 11:1).

It would not be considered a stretch to synonymously recognize the twelve as pastors since they were indeed shepherding and tending to this flock (Acts 20:28). Robert F. O'Toole infers that the apostles may have been influenced by the words of Jesus to be faithful and prudent managers, whom the master has put in charge because to whom much has been given, much will be required; words which O'Toole claims are only found in the book of Luke.[66] As pastors over this flock, they would not allow this problem to distract them from what they understood to be their God-ordained priorities as the leaders over this flock, devotion to prayer and ministry of the word. They needed to consistently be in contact with God so that they might properly minister to the flock of God through the word of God. As followers of Jesus Christ, we need to be influenced by those who understand their God-ordained priorities and are devoted to them.

The Apostle Paul testified, not once but twice, to the elders of the church in Ephesus that regardless to the trials that he had endured, he remained devoted to the priority of teaching the word of God (Acts 20:17-28) and he counseled the elders to do the same. The followers of Jesus Christ need to be influenced by those who are devoted to their God-ordained priorities and who provide the counsel to do the same. If we encounter those who are not devoted to God-ordained priorities and neither counsel others to do the same, then we should not allow ourselves to be influenced by them.

[66.] Peter F. O'Toole, "What Role Does Jesus' Saying in Acts 20,35 Play in Paul's Address to the Ephesian Elders?," *Biblica* 75, no. 3 (1994): 335-336, accessed August 28, 2020, ATLA Religion Database with ATLASerials, EBSCOhost.

Francois P. Viljoen reminds us that seeking the kingdom of God and His righteousness should be our first priority (Matthew 6:33).[67] Viljoen expresses that this positive command balances the prohibition of anxiety (Matthew 6:31) and fulfills the calling to exceed the righteousness of the scribes and the Pharisees (Matthew 5:20). The goal of the community of disciples is the establishment of God's kingdom and this goal is only reached by being devoted to our God-ordained priorities.[68]

Chuck Swindoll emphasizes that every decision of those who are trying to live out the kingdom life should be filtered through Matthew 6:33.[69] Since Matthew 6:33 represents the will of God, then Swindoll's thought can be expanded upon by saying that every decision should be filtered through God's will (Matthew 6:10, James 4:15). The revelation of God's will and His way is provided to us through His word (Deuteronomy 29:29) which explains the twelve's devotion to prayer and the ministry of the word.

To reiterate a statement made earlier in this chapter, the twelve needed to consistently be in contact with God so that they might properly minister to the flock of God through the word of God. The greatest influences upon our lives should be those who minister to us through God's word; not those who try to minister to us through worldly philosophies or human traditions (Colossians 2:8), but those who minister to us through God's word that His will might be done in our lives as we pursue God's purposes and not our own.

The beauty of the twelve's devotion and the problem that had arisen among the community of disciples is that God's word had already

---

[67] Francois P. Viljoen, "Righteousness and Identity Formation in the Sermon on the Mount," *Hervormde Teologiese Studies* 69, no. 1 (2013): 3, accessed May 23, 2020, ATLA Religion Database with ATLASerials, EBSCOhost.

[68] Viljoen, 8-9.

[69] Pastor Chuck Swindoll, "Priorities," Insight for Today: A Daily Devotional by Pastor Chuck Swindoll, The Bible-Teaching Ministry of Pastor Chuck Swindoll, accessed May 23, 2020, https://www.insight.org/resources/daily-devotional/individual/priorities.

provided the insight on how to deal with the problem of murmuring within the community of God's people. In Exodus 15:22-25, the children of Israel murmured against Moses because they had nothing to drink and could not drink the bitter waters of Marah. In Exodus 16:1-4, the children of Israel murmured once again because they had no food. In each instance, the solution to the murmuring was provided by God Himself. The twelve's devotion to prayer and the ministry of the word is what provided them with the answer to the problem of murmuring. Rather than trusting in themselves to determine a solution, the twelve looked to the Lord to provide the solution (Proverbs 3:5-8). Those who are an influence in our lives should be those who look to the Lord for the solutions to the problems that we encounter in this life, especially those that arise among the people of God.

Paul Overland argues for the intricate connection between Proverbs 3:1-12 and the Shema[70]; the Shema being the most essential prayer in all of Judaism which includes recitations from Deuteronomy 6:4-9; 11:13-21 and Numbers 15:37-41.[71] Overland surmises that loving God with all your heart and with all your soul is the advancement of one's devotion to God beyond all mental or physical longings.[72] The twelve's devotion to prayer and ministry of the word was a demonstration of their complete trust in the Lord to provide the solution to the problem of murmuring.

The solution that was provided by God through the twelve's devotion and ministry of the word was to equip the disciples with how to properly dispose of this issue that had arisen among them. The chosen word used to initially address the full number of disciples was brothers. The Thayer's Greek Lexicon defines this instance of brothers as a fellow

---

[70] Paul Overland, "Did the Sage Draw from the Shema? A Study of Proverbs 3:1-2," *The Catholic Biblical Quarterly* 62, no. 3 (Jul 2000): 424-440, accessed May 24, 2020, ATLA Religion Database with ATLASerials, EBSCOhost.

[71] "The Shema," My Jewish Learning, accessed May 24, 2020, https://www.myjewishlearning.com/article/the-shema.

[72] Overland, 428-431.

believer, united to another by the bond of affection.[73] In using the term brothers, the twelve were reminding the full number of disciples of their fellowship and the bond they should have with one another. The full number of disciples needed to be reminded of who they were as a single community. Even in this initial address, the Apostles were reminding them of their commonness and not their differences.

The twelve's involvement of the full number of disciples in the solution process was also indicative of a church having all things in common. If the church has a problem, then the problem should be a common problem. If the church has a common problem, then the whole church should be involved in the solution process. As followers of Jesus Christ, we should be under the influence of those who believe in more than just the commonality of all that is good in the church but also in the commonality of any issues that may arise in the church.

Some churches have the practice that only members who are considered to be "in good standing" (as defined by the church's by-laws) have the right to participate in decision making processes. If the early church had such a standard, then every member must have been "in good standing" because they all contributed to the common good of the church (Acts 4:32).

Dale has a chapter dedicated to resolving congregational conflicts.[74] Dale writes that there are generally two types of conflicts in the church, the first based on facts and the second based on feelings. Though most conflicts can be a blend of both types, one or the other will be predominant. Dale describes that factual controversies require cognitive resolution approaches which includes forming a problem solving task force, negotiating openly, and using consensus as a decision-making method to resolve the difficulty.[75] The issue of the Hellenistic widows being overlooked would definitely fall under the category of being a

---

[73]. "G80 – adelphos–Thayer's Greek Lexicon," Blue Letter Bible, accessed June 6, 2020, https://www.blueletterBible.org/lang/lexicon/lexicon.cfm?Strongs=G80&t=ESV.

[74]. Dale, chap. 13.

[75]. Dale, 159-160.

factual type of conflict (though feelings may also be inferred by the murmuring) and the twelve most definitely pursued the cognitive resolution techniques for resolving the difficulty.

The task given to the full number of disciples was to find seven men of good repute, full of the Holy Spirit and wisdom. Scholars seem to agree on the Biblical significance of the number seven, but the perspectives on its use in the context of this pericope seem to vary. Adam Clarke believes that the number seven was chosen so that there would be a superintendent for this business each day of the week.[76] This explanation seems the most viable since the problem was described as being one that had the potential of occurring daily.

Thayer defines good repute (or reputation) to be borne witness to or to be attested.[77] In other words, being full of the Holy Spirit and wisdom were to be characteristics which were well attested about these men among the full number of disciples. These men who were going to be appointed over the duty of making sure that the Hellenistic widows were no longer going to be neglected were also going to be an influence upon those to whom they would minister. Therefore, these men needed to be men who clearly demonstrated that they were full of the Spirit and wisdom. It should only be these such men who should be chosen to be leaders from among the followers of Jesus Christ because only these such men should be allowed to have such an influence.

In summary, the followers of Jesus Christ should only want people in their lives who will have a positive influence on their lives as opposed to those who will negatively influence them. Firstly, the more intimate relationships in the life of the follower of Jesus Christ should be those who have evidenced themselves to be disciples of Jesus Christ; those who are students of the word of God whose sincerest intention is to

---

[76.] Adam Clarke, "Commentaries: Adam Clarke – Acts 6:3." BIBLETOOLS, accessed July 16, 2019, https://www.Bibletools.org/index.cfm/fuseaction/Bible.show/sVerseID/27105/eVerseID/27105/RTD/Clarke.

[77.] "G3140 – martyreō–Thayer's Greek Lexicon," Blue Letter Bible, accessed June 6, 2020, https://www.blueletterBible.org/lang/lexicon/lexicon.cfm?Strongs=G3140&t=ESV.

acclimate their lives to what they have learned. Secondly, the more intimate relationships in the life of the follower of Jesus Christ should be those who exemplify and have a deep concern for maintaining unity among the community of the faithful; those who are sensitive to those things that threaten unity and are eager to pursue Biblical solutions when threats arise. Thirdly, the more intimate relationships in the life of the follower of Jesus Christ should be those who are devoted to the responsibilities that God has ordained for their lives; those who understand that what God has ordained for their lives is the priority for their lives and refuse to be distracted from it. Lastly, the more intimate relationships in the life of the follower of Jesus Christ should be those who believe in the commonality of the people of God; those who believe that problems that arise within the body of Christ are problems for us all and we must all be involved in the solution process. Those who are an influence on our lives should only be those who are striving to live a life that is godly.

CHAPTER THREE
Fulfilling God's Pleasure Purposes

Acts 6:5-7 (ESV)

⁵ And what they said pleased the whole gathering, and they chose Stephen, a man full of faith and of the Holy Spirit, and Philip, and Prochorus, and Nicanor, and Timon, and Parmenas, and Nicolaus, a proselyte of Antioch. ⁶ These they set before the apostles, and they prayed and laid their hands on them. ⁷ And the word of God continued to increase, and the number of the disciples multiplied greatly in Jerusalem, and a great many of the priests became obedient to the faith.

The continuing narrative that describes the solution to the problem of the neglected Hellenistic widows incited a common response from the whole gathering of disciples. The whole gathering was pleased with the twelve's counsel of choosing seven men full of the Spirit and wisdom (Acts 6:3). As those who were dedicated to adhering to the teachings that were derived from the word of God (the W. E. Vine definition of a disciple), contextually it can be surmised that the pleasure that was incited among the whole gathering was due to the solution being born out of the word of God; a revelation born out of the twelve's devotion to prayer and to the ministry of the word (Acts 6:2,

4).[78] When Biblical solutions to life's problems are revealed, then the common response among the followers of Jesus Christ should be one of pleasure.

The ultimate purpose for the followers of Jesus Christ is to please God (2 Corinthians 5:9). Thomas Aquinas insisted that unless we strive to please Him in this life, we will not be able to please Him or be present with Him in the other life.[79] Biblical solutions provide the certainty that God will be pleased.

Colossians 1:9-10 provides the principle that it is the knowledge of God's will that causes those who are faithful to Christ to live in a manner that is fully pleasing to Him. John W. Ritenbaugh interjects that this is not knowledge about God but it is the actual knowledge of God that is received through study and being taught.[80] When those who are faithful to Christ are provided with the knowledge of God's will, then the opportunity to please God comes with it. The opportunity to please God should ignite a pleasurable response within those who are faithful to Christ.

Psalm 1:1-2 emphasizes the delight that comes over those who are blessed by God when the counsel that they receive comes from the law of the Lord. King David described the gladness and the joy that came over him when he received counsel that came from the Lord (Psalm 16:7-11). The followers of Jesus Christ should be ecstatic when they receive solutions to life's problems that have been derived from the word of God because not only will they be blessed, but there will be an assurance that God will be pleased.

---

[78]. W. E. Vine, *Vine's Expository Dictionary of Old & New Testament Words*, (Nashville: Thomas Nelson Publishers, 1997), 308.

[79]. Thomas Aquinas, "Patristic Bible Commentary: St. Thomas Aquinas on 2 Corinthians: Chapter 5," accessed August 31, 2020, https://sites.google.com/site/aquinasstudybible/home/2-corinthians/st-thomas-aquinas-on-2-corinthians/chapter-1/chapter-2/chapter-3/chapter-4/chapter-5.

[80]. John W. Ritenbaugh, "Commentaries: Forerunner Commentary – Colossians 1:9-11," BIBLETOOLS, accessed June 18, 2020, https://www.bibletools.org/index.cfm/fuseaction/Bible.show/sVerseID/29475/eVerseID/29475.

Debbie Hunn notes the life altering transition that occurred in the life of the Apostle Paul because of the revelations that he received from God; the transition from a lifestyle of pleasing man to a lifestyle of pleasing God.[81] Every follower of Jesus Christ should have had the same life altering experience. The revelations that we receive from God's word that provide solutions to life's problems should incite pleasure because we know that the revelations from God's word are the solutions that please Him.

Pleasure with the solution that was derived from the word of God is indicative of agreement with God. What makes us the people of God is our agreement with God (Amos 3:3). Donald R. Sunukjian refers to this as an event that is inseparably connected.[82] It was agreement with God that led to the agreement among the whole gathering. Agreement among the whole gathering staved off the potential for division among them. It is agreement with the word of God amongst the people of God that diminishes the potential for schisms among the people of God.

In the Apostle Paul's appeal to the Corinthian church, he admonished them to bring an end to their quarreling because it had caused divisions within the church (1 Corinthians 1:10-11). John Chrysostom supplies that their oneness had perished.[83] When the people of God allow disagreements to cause division among them, then they are literally putting a gun to the head of their oneness. The solution that Paul presented to them was for them to agree with the enrichment of the knowledge that had been given to them in Christ. As followers of Jesus

---

[81] Debbie Hunn, "Pleasing God or Pleasing People? Defending the Gospel in Galatians 1-2," Biblica 91, no.1 (2010): 34-39, accessed June 22, 2020, ATLA Religion Database with ATLASerials, EBSCOhost.

[82] Donald R. Sunukjian, Bible Knowledge Commentary: An Exposition of the Scriptures by Dallas Seminary Faculty: Old Testament, ed. John F. Walvoord and Roy B. Zuck (n.p.: SP Publications, 1985), 1433.

[83] John Chrysostom, "Homilies of St. John Chrysostom, Archbishop of Constantinople, on the First Epistle of St. Paul the Apostle. To the Corinthians. – Homily III," Internet Sacred Test Archive, accessed September 1, 2020, https://www.sacred-texts.com/chr/ecf/112/1120007.htm.

Christ, if anything should cause us to agree it should be the enrichment of the knowledge, the wisdom, and the revelations that have been given to us in Jesus Christ.

It is hard to overlook the rhetoric used by the Apostle Paul in 1 Corinthians 1 to influence the thoughts of the Corinthians toward guarding against the potential of division. In Paul's greeting to the church, he reminds them that they were called to be "saints together" with everyone who calls upon the name of the Lord Jesus Christ (1 Corinthians 1:2). Paul pointed out that they were called into the "fellowship" of God's Son (1 Corinthians 1:9). Prior to Paul's appeal to the Corinthians to agree and be united, Paul calls them "brothers" (1 Corinthians 1:10). Paul's rhetoric throughout his admonishment to the Corinthian church emphasized unity and not division.

Ben Witherington III stresses that Paul's letters were rarely structured based on standard epistolary conventions.[84] Paul's letters were all structured from the very beginning to prepare the recipients for the message he was trying to convey.[85] The twelve in Acts 6 might be considered guilty of the same rhetorical prowess since they addressed the full number of disciples as "brothers" (Acts 6:2-3). This should speak volumes to those of us who claim to be followers of Jesus Christ to be cautious about the rhetoric that we use among ourselves because even our speech should be indicative of unity and not division. The very words that we speak should be pleasing to God, speech which stresses the unity that we should have with one another (Ephesians 4:25) and free from even a fragrance of division.

---

[84] Ben Witherington III, *New Testament Rhetoric: An Introductory Guide to the Art of Persuasion in and of the New Testament* (Eugene, OR: Cascade Books, 2009), 118, 112.

[85] Ibid., 112.

Mark Stirling observes that the way we speak to one another is indicative of our new humanity in Christ.[86] Stirling also points out that Ephesians 4:25 is indisputably a quotation from Zechariah 8:16 which commands us to speak those things that are true and make for peace.[87] As followers of Jesus Christ, the way that we speak to one another should be indicative of our new life in Christ. We should all be maturing by gaining a greater knowledge of God's word which is the truth (John 17: 17) so that we can speak truth to one another which also gains us the benefit of God's peace.

Raymond Apple refers to the happy (blessed) man as a man of action.[88] Those who are the blessed of God consider the counsel of God to be a call to service and action; a righteousness that needs to be more than just known, but a righteousness that needs to be performed.[89] The whole gathering acted upon the counsel that came from the word of God through the twelve and were able to choose seven that had the well-known reputation of being full of the Spirit and wisdom.

If the whole gathering were able to choose seven who were full of the Spirit, then that means that being full of the Spirit is detectable by those who are the disciples of Jesus Christ. God does not command the disciples of Jesus Christ to do anything that they are incapable of doing. Being full of the Spirit is detectable by the evidence that is consistently exuded by those who have God's Spirit.

Thomas O'Loughlin reminds us that not only is the Holy Spirit the unifier of God's people, but He also is the giver of diversity; a diversity

---

[86] Mark Stirling, "Transformed Walking and Missional Temple Building: Discipleship in Ephesians," *Presbyterion* 45, no. 2 (Fall 2019): 86, accessed September 7, 2020, ATLA Religion Database with ATLASerials, EBSCOhost.

[87] Ibid., 88.

[88] Raymond Apple, "The Happy Man of Psalms 1," *Jewish Bible Quarterly* 40, no. 3 (Jul-Sep 2012): 180, accessed July 3, 2020, ATLA Religion Database with ATLASerials, EBSCOhost.

[89] Ibid., 181.

that causes the mighty works of God to become known.[90] Following this train of thought one might say that the evidence exuded by those who are full of the Holy Spirit are also manifesting the mighty work that is being performed within them. The twelve were not only directing the whole gathering to choose seven who were full of the Spirit but the twelve were also providing them with the evidence of the Spirit's presence in their lives, the evidence of their wisdom.

Throughout the writings of Luke, being filled with the Spirit is evidenced by the things that were spoken. Being filled by the Spirit, Elizabeth exclaimed the blessing of the fruit of Mary's womb and how blessed Mary was among women because she believed in the fulfillment of what was spoken to her from the Lord (Luke 1:39-45). Zechariah being full of the Spirit prophesied about how God would use his son to be the forerunner of the coming Savior (Luke 1:67-79). On the day of Pentecost, the disciples who received the fullness of God's Spirit spoke in tongues as the Spirit gave them utterance (Acts 2:4) and those who heard the disciples heard them declaring the mighty works of God (Acts 2:11); things that would naturally be proclaimed in the respective countries of those who heard them.[91] Those who were with Peter and John after being filled with the Holy Spirit spoke the word of God with boldness (Acts 4:31).

Within these examples, Luke is demonstrating that God glorifying speech is evidentiary of being filled with the Spirit of God. If we want to please God with the choices that we make of those who are being considered to be leaders among us, then the evidence that we should look for should be the wisdom by which they speak. 1 Corinthians 12:8 defines this gift as the utterance of wisdom; the God given ability to

---

[90.] Thomas O'Loughlin, "The Diversifying Spirit: The Gift of Pentecost," The Pastoral Review 11, no. 3 (May-Jun 2015): 4, 7, accessed September 2, 2020, ATLA Religion Database with ATLASerials, EBSCOhost.

[91.] Adam Clarke, "The Adam Clarke Commentary: Chapter 2," StudyLight. org., accessed September 7, 2020, http://classic.studylight.org/com/acc/view.cgi?book=ac&chapter=002.

reason by use of the wisdom that God has provided in His word. Truth that has been persuasively set forth to work conversion among those who really hear it.[92]

Ephesians 5:15-17 equates wisdom with the knowledge of the will of the Lord. Shane Berg calls the will of God the crucial knowledge that all humans need.[93] Therefore, it would not be farfetched to consider that the whole gathering was looking for seven men who had the well-known reputation of speaking up when it came to the will of the Lord being done. The main character of our particular focus, Philip who would become known as the evangelist, was identified with those who had the well-known reputation for speaking up when it came to the will of God being done. If we want God to be pleased, then as followers of Jesus Christ we should all want to be identified with those who have the well-known reputation for speaking up when it comes to the will of God being done.

Itamar Kislev reasons from the story of the twelve spies [Numbers 13-14] that God Himself showed up to protect Caleb and Joshua from being stoned by the whole congregation of Israelites because Caleb and Joshua advocated for the will of God being done.[94] If Kislev's reasoning is correct, then this should be a motivator for the followers of Jesus Christ to always be willing to speak up for the will of God being done knowing that God Himself will protect them from those who might even violently oppose them (2 Thessalonians 3:3).

Not only were Caleb and Joshua protected by God, but they were also the only two in their generation that did not fall in the wilderness

---

[92.] "Pulpit Commentary," Bible Hub, accessed September 6, 2020, https://biblehub.com/commentaries/pulpit/1_corinthians/12.htm.

[93.] Shane Berg, "Ben Sira, the Genesis Creation Accounts, and the Knowledge of God's Will," *Journal of Biblical Literature* 132, no. 1 (2013): 139, accessed September 6, 2020, ATLA Religion Database with ATLASerials, EBSCOhost.

[94.] Itamar Kislev, "Joshua (and Caleb) in the Priestly Spies Story and Joshua's Initial Appearance in the Priestly Source: A Contribution to an Assessment of the Pentateuchal Priestly Material," *Journal of Biblical Literature* 136, no. 1 (2017): 48, accessed July 8, 2020, ATLA Religion Database with ATLASerials, EBSCOhost.

because they chose to please God by speaking up for His will being done (Numbers 14:30). When the follower of Jesus Christ chooses to please God by persisting for His will being done, they will be free from the chastisement that falls upon those who do not.

Stanley D. Toussaint observes that the names of the seven men who were chosen were Greek names and that the early church evidently felt that the problem of the neglected Hellenistic widows would best be solved by those who were Hellenists themselves.[95] The flaw in believing this to be true is that it adds to the criteria provided by the twelve of choosing seven men that had the well-known reputation of being full of the Spirit and wisdom. If the early church felt that this was the criteria that was revealed to them through prayer and the ministry of the word, then they would not have added to the criteria that was provided to them from God's word. Those of us who are dedicated to the things that God has said should be on guard against adding any additional criteria to it because this has the potential of being displeasing to God.

Proverbs 30:5-6 teaches us that every word of God proves itself to be true and those who add to it open themselves up to the rebuke of God. Various other versions of Scripture translate Proverbs 30:5a as every word of God being pure. Bryan Murphy states that this conveys that the word of God is refined, purified, or unmixed; fully cleansed of any and all impurities.[96] As followers of Jesus Christ and those who wholly believe in the word that has come from God, this should also express how we feel about God's word; that it should remain unmixed and fully cleansed of any and all impurities especially from those things that we might consider should be added to it. Christine Roy Yoder describes an "added-to" word from God as being both a muddied and distorted

---

[95.] Stanley D. Toussaint, *Bible Knowledge Commentary: An Exposition of the Scriptures by Dallas Seminary Faculty: New Testament Edition*, ed. John F. Walvoord and Roy B. Zuck (Colorado Springs: ChariotVictor Publishing, 1983), 367.

[96.] Bryan Murphy, "The Unalterable Word," The Master's Seminary Journal 26, no. 2 (Fall 2015): 171, accessed September 4, 2020, ATLA Religion Database with ATLASerials, EBSCOhost.

truth.[97] Those of us who believe that God's word is pure and that it proves itself to be true, should have no desire to muddy or distort the truths that exist in God's word by adding to it. Fear of the rebuke of God should be the motivator that keeps us from doing so.

For those of us who remember the old TV show, Lost in Space, we should remember the flailing arms of the robot while he shouted, "danger Will Robinson." This same imagery should pop up in the minds of the follower of Jesus Christ when we attempt to make observations that do not completely line up with the word of God. There is the possibility of placing ourselves in danger of being rebuked by God for adding to what He has already proven to be true and pure. The precepts of the Lord are what have been proven trustworthy and they are what should be performed with faithfulness and uprightness (Psalm 111:7-8), not any worldly wisdom that we deem necessary to add (1 Corinthians 3:19).

The seven men who were chosen might be considered as those who stood out from among the multitude of disciples because of the gift of wisdom that God had given to them, according to His sovereign will.[98] Therefore, what the congregation of followers was looking for were those who had the gift to perform the task. If the followers of Jesus Christ want God to be pleased with those who have been chosen to perform a particular task among them, then what they should be looking for is more than just those who are willing but those who possess the gift for accomplishing the task.

When Moses was tasked with building the tabernacle, God directed Moses to those who possessed the gifts for performing the work, those who had been filled with the Spirit of God (Exodus 31:1-11). Matthew

---

[97] Christine Roy Yoder, "On the Threshold of Kingship: A Study of Agur (Proverbs 30)," *Interpretation* 63, no. 3, (Jul 2009): 261, accessed September 4, 2020, ATLA Religion Database with ATLASerials, EBSCOhost.

[98] Walter J. Bartling, "The Congregation of Christ – A Charismatic Body: An Exegetical Study of 1 Corinthians 12," *Concordia Theological Monthly* 40, no. 2 (Feb 1969): 75, accessed July 14, 2020, ATLA Religion Database with ATLASerials, EBSCOhost.

Henry identifies that it was God Himself who qualified these persons for this service.[99] Just like Moses, the followers of Jesus Christ should be asking God to clearly identify those who have the gift for accomplishing the task, those whom He has qualified for the service. 1 Corinthians 12 infers that it is by the manifestation of the spiritual gifts that God has given us that set us apart from paganistic and idolatrous practices. We please God when we take full advantage of the gifts that He has given to the church, gifts that set us apart, to accomplish the tasks that He has set before us.

Bartling insists that identifying and exercising the spiritual gifts that God has given the church is an acknowledgment of the Lordship of Jesus Christ.[100] It is by those gifts that Christ sets us to task in the body of Christ and empowers us to act.[101] Following this train of thought, one might even postulate that the twelve already had an inkling of who the seven were whom God had gifted to fulfill the ministry of assuring that the Hellenistic widows were no longer overlooked. The criteria given to the congregation gave them the opportunity to exercise the ability of identifying those who had been gifted by God for this specific task.

The pericope being examined in this chapter identifies the twelve as the apostles. Richard B. Hays draws our attention to the Jewish rhetorical device, gezerah shawah, which he defines as catchword linkages between two texts.[102] The catchword linkages are intended to imply a contextual similarity in application. The catchword linkage between this pericope and the one examined in the previous chapter of this writing project is "the twelve" and "the apostles."

[99.] Matthew Henry, Commentary on the Whole Bible by Matthew Henry, ed. Rev. Leslie F. Church, Ph.D., F.R.Hist.S. (Grand Rapids: Zondervan Publishing House), 105.

[100.] Bartling, 67.

[101.] Ibid., 69.

[102.] Richard B. Hays, *Echoes of Scripture in the Letters of Paul* (New Haven: Yale University Press, 1989): 13.

In this context, the author Luke may be using the term apostle as an echo of the term's previous uses, such as Luke 6:12-16; 9:1-6,10, which are Luke's first mentions of the term apostle. Through this nomenclature change from the twelve to the apostles, it is quite possible that Luke is reminding us of the twelve's familiarity with being standouts who were also chosen and gifted for a particular task. The twelve/apostles were empowered and given authority by Christ over all demons and diseases and commanded to proclaim the kingdom of God. The apostles are described by Robert Duncan Culver as ministers plenipotentiary due to the high level of authority passed down to them by Christ.[103] Whereas the seven, were empowered with wisdom by God's Spirit to oversee the ministry of the neglected widows.

It is God's good pleasure to empower His people for the tasks that glorify His name and are beneficial for the building up of His church (Philippians 2:13). The followers of Jesus Christ should always find pleasure with the things that please God.

Neither group, the apostles nor the seven, signed up for their ministries but were chosen based on the God given gifts that they possessed. This might account for the weaknesses of the church today. We may be weakening the church by allowing people to work in ministries that they may not have been chosen for nor empowered by God to perform. Bartling surmises that each of us has been charismatically endowed by God's Spirit and we should be functioning from our gifts.[104] The power of the church is revealed when the followers of Jesus Christ are functioning in the areas for which they have been gifted. This is what pleases God and acknowledges Christ's lordship over us.

The seven that were chosen to oversee the ministry of the neglected widows were set before the apostles who then prayed and laid their hands on them. The laying on of hands is considered to be one of the

---

[103] Robert Duncan Culver, "Apostles and the Apostolate in the New Testament," *Bibliotheca sacra* 134, no. 534 (Apr-Jun): 136, accessed September 8, 2020, ATLA Religion Database with ATLASerials, EBSCOhost.

[104] Bartling, 76-77.

elementary principles within the doctrines of Christ and should be well understood by those who are pursuing the pleasure of God that they might go on to maturity (Hebrews 6:1-2).

Martin G. Collins summarizes the laying on of hands as symbolizing the bestowal of blessings, authority, and distinctiveness; the symbolic act designed to represent a person being set apart by God for a holy use.[105] Moses was commanded to take the Levites from among the people of Israel and after being ritualistically cleansed, have all the people of Israel lay their hands on them because they had been chosen by God to do service unto Him (Numbers 8:5-11). Likewise, Moses was commanded to lay hands on Joshua and commission him in the sight of all of Israel to succeed Moses as their shepherd (Numbers 27:12-23). After fasting and praying, hands were laid on Barnabas and Saul because they had been set apart by the Holy Spirit to do the work that He had called them to do (Acts 13:1-3). The commonality of these occurrences is that hands were laid on those whom God had chosen for the specific tasks to which they had been specifically called.

W. Sibley Towner describes the Jewish hermeneutical device, *Binyan °av, as* establishing comparability between laws. It is based on the presence of similar obligations in several laws of the Torah being derived from factors which all share in common.[106] More simply put, if similar phraseology is found in multiple Scriptures, then what is found in one is applicable to all. Applying this hermeneutic to the apostles' laying on of hands upon the seven with those described in the previous paragraph, this would cause the apostle's act to represent the pleasure and agreement of God with those who had been chosen, especially since prayer was rendered prior to the laying on of hands in pursuit of God's

---

[105.] Martin G. Collins, "Basic Doctrines: The Laying on of Hands," BIBLETOOLS, accessed July 20, 2020, https://www.bibletools.org/index.cfm/fuseaction/Library.sr/CT/BS/k/235/Basic-Doctrines-Laying-On-of-Hands.htm.

[106.] W. Sibley Towner, "Hermeneutical Systems of Hillel and the Tannaim: A Fresh Look," *Hebrew Union College Annual* 53, (1982): 18, accessed July 21, 2020, ATLA Religion Database with ATLASerials, EBSCOhost.

divine favor. As followers of Jesus Christ, we should want God to be pleased with the choices that we make, especially with those who have been chosen to be servant leaders among us.

The fruit of the apostles' solution of allowing the seven to oversee the ministry of the neglected widows so that they might remain devoted to prayer and to the ministry of the word is that the word of God continued to increase. This increase resulted in the number of disciples multiplying. The increase was not only the result of the apostles remaining devoted to prayer and to the ministry of the word, but it was also the result of the compassion that was demonstrated to the neglected widows.

Patrick J. Hartin discusses the collectivist mindset of those who lived in the first century Mediterranean society; a mindset more concerned for the group than the individual.[107] Attributes of those who lived in this collectivist culture included adherence to the norms that guide the group and the value of preserving harmony.[108] It was the outward demonstration of this same type of mindset within this community of disciples that resulted in the word of God continuing to increase. The ministry of the church has to be more than just devotion to prayer and the ministry of the word, but the ministry of the church should also include demonstrations of compassion toward its membership. As followers of Jesus Christ, God expects His people to be a people of compassion. God is pleased when His children are tenderhearted toward one another (Ephesians 4:32) and when they have compassionate hearts as God's chosen ones (Colossians 3:12).

Contextually, Ephesians 4:32 has a dependency upon Ephesians 4:30 which commands us not to grieve the Holy Spirit. The commandments which follow Ephesians 4:30 are intended to keep us from doing just that. C. Mack Roark labels these commandments as the antidote

---

[107] Patrick J. Hartin, Paul's Social Network: Brothers and Sisters in Faith: Apollos: Paul's Partner or Rival? ed. Bruce J. Malina (Collegeville, Minnesota: Liturgical Press), 20-45.

[108] Ibid., 26.

for grieving the Holy Spirit.[109] Therefore, if we are tenderhearted and compassionate toward one another then God is pleased and not grieved.

In summary, one of the things that should incite pleasure within the followers of Jesus Christ should be when solutions to life's problems are born out of the word of God. This incitement of pleasure should be aroused within us because solutions that are derived from the word of God are those that provide the certainty that God will be pleased. Not only will God be pleased, but solutions that are derived from the word of God provide the optimal opportunity for agreement amongst the people of God. Once these solutions become known then they need to be more than just known, they need to be acted upon. God does not provide us with solutions for them just to be known. God intends for the solutions that He has provided to be acted upon.

When choosing leaders to oversee ministries that serve the people of God, we need to choose leaders with whom God will be pleased. Leaders who have been gifted by God for the task, especially those who are unafraid to stand up for the will of God being done. The main motivation for the follower of Jesus Christ in all situations and in all circumstances should be to please God (2 Corinthians 5:9).

[109.] C. Mack Roark, "Interpreting Ephesians 4-6: God's People in a Walk Worthy of His Calling," *Southwestern Journal of Theology* 39, no.1 (Fall 1996): 37, accessed July 26, 2020, ATLA Religion Database with ATLASerials, EBSCOhost.

CHAPTER FOUR
Fulfilling God's Exemplary Purposes

Acts 6:8-15 (ESV)

⁸ And Stephen, full of grace and power, was doing great wonders and signs among the people. ⁹ Then some of those who belonged to the synagogue of the Freedmen (as it was called), and of the Cyrenians, and of the Alexandrians, and of those from Cilicia and Asia, rose up and disputed with Stephen. ¹⁰ But they could not withstand the wisdom and the Spirit with which he was speaking. ¹¹ Then they secretly instigated men who said, "We have heard him speak blasphemous words against Moses and God." ¹² And they stirred up the people and the elders and the scribes, and they came upon him and seized him and brought him before the council, ¹³ and they set up false witnesses who said, "This man never ceases to speak words against this holy place and the law, ¹⁴ for we have heard him say that this Jesus of Nazareth will destroy this place and will change the customs that Moses delivered to us." ¹⁵ And gazing at him, all who sat in the council saw that his face was like the face of an angel.

In the previous chapter, Stephen was identified as one of the seven standouts that were chosen to oversee the ministry of the neglected

Hellenistic widows. The criteria for selecting the seven was that they should have the well-known reputation for being full of the Spirit and wisdom. Scripture reveals that not only was Stephen filled with the Holy Spirit and wisdom, but he was also full of faith, grace, and power (Acts 6:5, 8); descriptors that depict someone totally immersed in the cause in which they believe.[110] Stephen even stood out among those who were considered standouts themselves. One might say that Stephen was an exemplary disciple of Jesus Christ.

Stephen is described by Charles Harris Nash as the model layman.[111] Philip (our focus character for this study), like Stephen, was also considered a standout among the disciples in the early church. God specifically placed Philip in direct association with Stephen, someone who was even more of a standout than himself. On this journey to fulfilling the purposes of God, we need to associate with those who demonstrate themselves to be exemplary examples of what the Lord Jesus Christ would have us to be.

Nash states that the best biography of the best people is the best character food for those who desire and firmly purpose to be their own best for God.[112] As followers of Jesus Christ, our heart's desire should be to be our best for God. The fulfillment of that desire is aided by associating with those who consistently demonstrate the godly characteristics that we ourselves should aspire to exude so that we might feed off of them. Though we may not be able to obtain the sinless perfection of Jesus Christ Himself, Stephen shows us what a sinner saved by

---

[110] Steven A. Hamon, "Beyond Self-actualization: Comments on the Life and Death of Stephen the Martyr," *Journal of Psychology & Theology* 5, no. 4 (Fall 1977): 292, accessed September 18, 2020, ATLA Religion Database with ATLASerials, EBSCOhost.

[111] Charles Harris Nash, "Stephen, the Model Layman: The Unique, Transcendent Image of Jesus in Life and Death, 'Filled with all the Fulness of God.' Acts 6-7," *Review & Expositor* 23, no. 4 (Oct 1926): 452, accessed September 15, 2020, ATLA Religion Database with ATLASerials, EBSCOhost.

[112] Ibid., 452.

grace may become.[113] Just like God provided Philip with the exemplary example of Stephen, we should seek out those whom God has provided among ourselves who demonstrate themselves to be exemplary.

Daniel and the three Hebrew boys were the standouts among those who were taken from Jerusalem when Nebuchadnezzar besieged it, but it was Daniel who resolved not to defile himself with the king's food or wine (Daniel 1:3-6, 8). Daniel is described more than once in Scripture as having an excellent spirit (Daniel 5:12, 6:3). Donald C. Polaski insists that contextually this description of Daniel was intentionally meant to be a contrast to those in the Chaldean court.[114] As followers of Jesus Christ, God has called us to be a contrast to those who live ungodly so that others might get a glimpse of what a true follower of Jesus Christ looks like.

Because of the three Hebrew boys' decision to associate themselves with Daniel's choice not to defile himself with the king's food or wine, the three Hebrew boys were also blessed of God to receive learning and skill in all literature and wisdom (Daniel 1:17). The blessings of God can be found in associating ourselves with those who are exemplary. Those who are satisfied with just being mediocre Christians are no benefit to those who are on the journey of achieving God's exemplary purpose in their lives. The greatest benefits are found when we are in the company of those who are exemplary.

God has called us to excel in everything. The Apostle Paul teaches that excellence is inspired by the example of others (2 Corinthians 8:7). If the follower of Jesus Christ desires to achieve God's exemplary purpose in their own lives, then they need to be in the company of those who are exemplary. Stephen Joubert emphasizes that excellence is the

---

[113.] Ibid., 453.

[114.] Donald C. Polaski, "Mene, Mene, Tekel, Parsin: Writing and Resistance in Daniel 5 and 6," *Journal of Biblical Literature* 123, no. 4 (Wint 2004): 656, accessed September 16, 2020, ATLA Religion Database with ATLASerials, EBSCOhost.

mark of a mature believer.[115] God has commanded the followers of Jesus Christ to go on to maturity (Hebrews 6:1) and the pursuit of maturity must have excellence in its sights.

The characteristics that caused Stephen to be a standout even among the others who were standouts were the fullness of faith, the fullness of grace, and power; in addition, to being full of the Spirit and wisdom. John O. Reid in his article on continuing faith defines faith as a belief that galvanizes into a conviction that will produce righteous works.[116] Maybe this offers an explanation for the great signs and wonders that were being performed by Stephen. The fullness of his conviction resulted in the galvanization of great signs and wonders.

Through the apostles, the necessity of being associated with those who are exemplary rears its beautiful head because the apostles who were fully dedicated to what God had called them to do were performing signs and wonders regularly among the people (Acts 2:43; 5:12). Signs and wonders that gained the apostles a prestige and notoriety that eclipsed the high priest and the Sadducees.[117]

Contextually it's hard not to conclude that it was the apostles' exemplary example that influenced Stephen to be all that he could be. Maybe this is why we are not provided with the details of what the signs and wonders were that Stephen had performed because the main point was not the signs and wonders but the influence of being associated with those who were exemplary.

---

[115]. Stephen Joubert, "Behind the Mask of Rhetoric: 2 Corinthians 8 and the Intratextual Relation Between Paul and the Corinthians," *Neotestamentica* 26, no. 1 (1992): 107, accessed September 21, 2020, ATLA Religion Database with ATLASerials, EBSCOhost.

[116]. John O. Reid, "What the Bible Says About Continuing in the Faith," BIBLETOOLS, accessed September 16, 2020, https://www.bibletools.org/index.cfm/fuseaction/topical.show/RTD/cgg/ID/8552/Continuing-in-Faith.htm.

[117]. Timothy W. Reardon, "'Hanging on a Tree': Deuteronomy 21.22-13 and the Rhetoric of Jesus' Crucifixion in Acts 5.12-42," *Journal for the Study of the New Testament* 37, no. 4 (Jun 2015): 423, accessed September 29, 2020, ATLA Religion Database with ATLASerials, EBSCOhost.

One has to also consider if the writer Luke was intentionally contrasting the faith of Stephen to the faith of the priests (Acts 6:7). Stephen is described as being full of faith, whereas the priests are described as those who became obedient to the faith. Was it the writer Luke's intention to direct our understanding in there being a difference between being full of faith and being obedient to the faith?

Handley Dunelm discusses the traceable meanings found in Scripture for faith.[118] His study determined that the overwhelming majority of cases for the meaning of faith convey reliance and trust. Whereas, another line of meaning conveys the sense of an orthodox belief or creedal confession.[119] It seems quite plausible that Luke may have been suggesting that what the priests had done were to make a creedal confession of faith, but Stephen had placed his full reliance and trust in the Christian faith. The expressions used to describe Stephen verses those used to describe the priests may have been intended to rhetorically contrast Stephen as being exemplary. Our relationship with Jesus Christ should be more than just based on our creedal confessions. Our creedal confessions should only mark the beginning of our faith. Our relationship with Christ should be exemplified by our full reliance and trust in Him (Proverbs 3:5).

The predominant definition of grace is favor; the favorable inclinations of a superior towards the inferior.[120] The characteristics of being full of faith and full of grace may be representative of the reciprocating relationship between Stephen being the inferior and the Lord Jesus Christ, the ultimate Superior. Because Stephen placed his full reliance and trust (faith) in Christ, the Lord Jesus Christ blessed Stephen with the fullness of His favor (grace). As followers of Jesus Christ, we should

---

[118.] Handley Dunelm, "The Meaning of Faith of Faith in the Bible," BIBLETOOLS, accessed September 18, 2020, https://www.bibletools.org/index.cfm/fuseaction/Def.show/RTD/ISBE/ID/3349/Faith.htm.

[119.] Ibid.

[120.] G.G. Findlay, *Hastings' Dictionary of the Bible*, ed. James Hastings (Harrington DE: Delmarva Publications, 2014), Kindle.

want more than just a few crumbs of God's grace. We should desire the fulness of His grace which only comes to those who are exemplary.

The Apostle Paul emphasizes that spiritual gifts are the evidence of God's grace given to those who are being sanctified in Christ as a confirmation of being in right relationship with God the Father and the Lord Jesus Christ (1 Corinthians 1:1-6). The Expositor's Greek Testament equates being sanctified in Christ as more than just receiving salvation, but actually living a life that is fully devoted to God.[121] To receive the fullness of God's grace, the follower of Jesus Christ needs to do more than just be the recipient of salvation, the follower of Jesus Christ should strive to be exemplary.

The phrase "full of grace" seems to only be found in one other place in our English translations, John 1:14. This fullness of grace is only similarly associated with the glory that was beheld in the only (begotten) Son who came from the Father, the Word that had become flesh. This is the testimony of those who experienced Christ's uniqueness.[122] If the fullness of grace is a specific descriptive of the Word that had become flesh, then it seems to be reasonable that the allusion, as it refers to Stephen, is that Stephen had allowed the word to become flesh in his own life. As a disciple of Jesus Christ, Stephen was living what he had heard from God's word. He was more than a hearer; he was a doer of the word (James 1:22). The type of exemplary examples that the followers of Jesus Christ should be directly associated with are those who are living what they have heard from the word of God.

This unique similarity between Jesus Christ and the exemplary example provided for us in Stephen may account for the only time that the Scriptures tell us that the Son of Man was standing at the right hand of God (Acts 7:56). Charles Box provides that Stephen saw Jesus

---

[121.] "Expositor's Greek Testament," Bible Hub, accessed September 29, 2020, https://biblehub.com/commentaries/egt/1_corinthians/1.htm.

[122.] Gordon D. Kirchhevel, "The Children of God and the Glory that John 1:14 Saw," *Bulletin of Biblical Research* 6, (1996): 89, accessed October 5, 2020, ATLA Religion Database with ATLASerials, EBSCOhost.

standing as his Advocate.[123] If the follower of Jesus Christ wants to see Jesus standing as their Advocate in this life, then the pursuit is to be exemplary.

Luke returns our focus to the wisdom and the Spirit that Stephen possessed (Acts 6:10). It was the wisdom and the Spirit with which Stephen spoke that caused him to withstand those who rose up from the synagogue to dispute with him. The same gift which identified Stephen as one of the standouts to be utilized by God in the ministry of the neglected Hellenistic widows was the same gift that enabled him to withstand those who rose up against him. Through Stephen's ministry and his ability to withstand those who rose up to dispute with him, it becomes obvious that the gifts which God has given us through His Spirit are not intended to be utilized in just one particular way but are to be utilized as occasion dictates. This is the exemplary way of the followers of Jesus Christ.

The provision of wisdom, which no adversary will be able to withstand, is the fulfillment of the promise given by Jesus Christ to those who take advantage of the opportunity to be a witness to their persecutors (Luke 21:10-15). William D. Shiell refers to this promise as the enablement to speak prudently when standing trial for your faith.[124] To those of us who desire to be exemplary, it should be comforting to know that it is not incumbent upon ourselves to determine what should be said to our persecutors but God Himself will give us the words and wisdom with which to reply (Luke 12:11-12). Our dependency should be completely upon Him in the face of persecution.

The word synagogue as used in Acts 6:9 is used in the singular sense which seems to designate a single place frequented by the

---

[123.] Charles Box, "Bible Commentaries: Charles Box's Commentaries on Selected books of the Bible: Acts 7," Studylight.org, 2014, https://www.studylight.org/commentaries/box/acts-7.html.

[124.] William D. Shiell, "'I Will Give You a Mouth and Wisdom'; Prudent Speech in Luke 21:15," *Review & Expositor* 112, no. 4 (Nov 2015): 609, accessed October 13, 2020, ATLA Religion Database with ATLASerials, EBSCOhost.

various persons mentioned, but the existence of so many synagogues in Jerusalem at that time has led many scholars to suppose that two or more synagogues are in view.[125] Debating the number of synagogues may be distracting to Luke's point. Though the odds were against Stephen in number, learning, and possibly social position, the opposition were still not able to resist the wisdom and the Spirit by which Stephen spoke.[126] When the follower of Jesus Christ's dependency is fully upon God, then they are never outnumbered.

Archeological evidence has been discovered revealing that priests served in the synagogues. The Dura-Europa synagogue, unearthed in Syria in November of 1932, mentions a priest among the leaders of the synagogue in the Dura dedication inscription.[127] A list of priestly courses was also found painted on the columns of this same synagogue.[128] This may establish a contextual motivation for the dispute that rose up between Stephen and those of the synagogue since Luke tells us that a great many of the priests became obedient to the faith (Acts 6:7). Hamon suggests that the ministry of Stephen had expanded from not only serving as an overseer of the neglected Hellenistic widows, but to also include entering the synagogue to be a witness of the One in

---

[125] James Burton Coffman, "Bible Commentaries: Coffman Commentaries on the Bible: Acts 6," Studylight.org, accessed September 30, 2020, https://www.studylight.org/commentaries/bcc/acts-6.html.

[126] J. W. McGarvey, "Bible Commentaries: McGarvey's Original Commentary on Acts: Acts 6," Studylight.org, accessed September 30, 2020, https://www.studylight.org/commentaries/oca/acts-6.html.

[127] Elias Joseph Bickerman, "Symbolism in the Dura Synagogue," *Harvard Theological Review* 58, no. 1 (Jan 1965): 127, accessed October 13, 2020, ATLA Religion Database with ATLASerials, EBSCOhost.; Kara L. Schenk, "Temple, Community, and Sacred Narrative in the Dura-Europos Synagogue," *AJS Review* 34, no. 2 (Nov 2010): 198, accessed October 13, 2020, ATLA Religion Database with ATLASerials, EBSCOhost.

[128] Fergus Millar, "Inscriptions, Synagogues and Rabbis in Late Antique Palestine," *Journal for the Study of Judaism* 42, no. 2 (2011): 272, accessed October 10, 2020, ATLA Religion Database with ATLASerials, EBSCOhost.

Whom he believed.[129] This also provides an enhancement to our understanding of why Saul specifically asked for letters to the synagogues of Damascus in search of any belonging to the Way (Acts 9:1-2). God used the wisdom and the Spirit that He had given Stephen to draw the priests to the Christian faith. As those who are aspiring to follow the exemplary example of Stephen, our heart's desire should be that God use us to draw others to the Christian faith.

Jesus Himself said that no one comes to Him unless the Father who sent Him draws them through the things that they have been taught by God. If someone really hears what is being taught and is willing to learn from it, then they will come to Christ (John 6:44-45). Dieter Mitternacht expresses that these verses emphasize the role of God the Father in the ministry of Jesus Christ.[130] Those who are aspiring for excellence in Christ should allow themselves to be used of God to teach others His will in the hopes that those being taught might be drawn to God (Matthew 28:19-20).

Not to be outdone, those who disputed with Stephen secretly instigated false witnesses against Him which stirred up the people, including their leadership. The focus for those who are pursuing the excellence that God has commanded should not be on the instigation of the false witnesses, but on how Stephen responded. Jesus has already warned us that we will be reviled, persecuted, and have all kinds of evil uttered against us falsely (Matthew 5:11). Rachel L. Coleman directs us back to Matthew 5:10 reminding us that we are citizens of the kingdom of heaven whose orientation is toward righteousness.[131] Since our orientation is in contradiction to those who still reside in the domain of

---

[129.] Hamon, 292.

[130.] Dieter Mitternacht, "Knowledge-making and Myth-making in John 6: A Narrative-Psychological Reading," *Svensk Exegetisk Arsbok* 72, (2007): 59, accessed October 14, 2020, ATLA Religion Database with ATLASerials, EBSCOhost.

[131.] Rachel L. Coleman, "The Lukan Beatitudes (Luke 6.20–26) in the Canonical Choir: A 'Test Case' for John Christopher Thomas' Hermeneutical Proposal," *Journal of Pentecostal Theology* 26, no. 1 (2017): 63, accessed October 14, 2020, ATLA Religion Database with ATLASerials, EBSCOhost.

darkness, then the occurrence of false accusations should not take the followers of Jesus Christ by surprise. The focus should not be on those who falsely accused Stephen, but on how Stephen responded. The first response which is provided by the lectionary focus of this chapter is the look upon Stephen's face; his face was like the face of an angel.

Among the various scholarly perspectives on what is meant by Stephen's face having the appearance of an angel, those which align with the one provided by Barton W. Johnson seem the more credible. Johnson's inclination is toward Stephen's face being radiant with his own divinely inspired peace and not with what some consider to be a supernatural splendor, especially since his visage did not inspire any awe from the council.[132] Stephen had a peace that surpassed their understanding (Philippians 4:7) and it shown upon his face. Stephen is the exemplary demonstration of how the peace of Christ ruled in his heart (Colossians 3:15) and not the trouble he was currently facing (John 14:27). Denise M. Massey describes this peace as a deep and abiding peace which is even beyond our own comprehension.[133]

Philippians 4:6-7 is like a GPS that gives us directions to travel from anxiety to peace.[134] On the journey to being exemplary, we will have anxious moments, but that does not mean that we have to stay in the moment. Prayers lifted up with thanksgiving move us out of anxious moments into an incomprehensible peace. When we refuse to place too much thought on those things that cause us anxiety and become practitioners of what we have learned, received, heard, and seen from the exemplary examples that God has provided for us, then the God of peace will be with us (Philippians 4:8-9) causing us to have His peace.

[132.] Barton W. Johnson, "Bible Commentaries: People's New Testament: Acts 6," Studylight.org, accessed October 16, 2020, https://www.studylight.org/commentaries/pnt/acts-6.html.

[133.] Denise M. Massey, "A Word About: Praying When You are Afraid (Phil 4:6-7)," *Review & Expositor* 115, no. 2 (2018): 268, accessed October 19, 2020, ATLA Religion Database with ATLASerials, EBSCOhost.

[134.] Ibid.

As followers of Jesus Christ, our goal should be to follow Stephen's exemplary example and not let any type of trouble have rulership over our hearts, but let the peace that Christ has given us take its proper place in our lives.

In summary, our goal on this Christian journey should be to become exemplary. God did not call us to be mediocre, but to pursue excellence. To aid us in this pursuit, we should seek out those whom God has provided among us who demonstrate themselves to be exemplary. God's desire for us is to contrast and be a witness to those who live ungodly that they might get a glimpse of what a true follower of Jesus Christ looks like and hopefully be drawn to Christ. This only occurs when we are fully convicted to what we say we believe as an exemplification of our full reliance and trust in the God that we say we serve. When the follower of Jesus Christ allows the word of God to become flesh in their own lives and remain fully dedicated to it, then the result will be the blessings of God and the fullness of His favor.

CHAPTER FIVE
Fulfilling God's Responsive Purposes

1 Peter 3:8-17 (ESV)

⁸ Finally, all of you, have unity of mind, sympathy, brotherly love, a tender heart, and a humble mind. ⁹ Do not repay evil for evil or reviling for reviling, but on the contrary, bless, for to this you were called, that you may obtain a blessing. ¹⁰ For "Whoever desires to love life and see good days, let him keep his tongue from evil and his lips from speaking deceit; ¹¹ let him turn away from evil and do good; let him seek peace and pursue it. ¹² For the eyes of the Lord are on the righteous, and his ears are open to their prayer. But the face of the Lord is against those who do evil." ¹³ Now who is there to harm you if you are zealous for what is good? ¹⁴ But even if you should suffer for righteousness› sake, you will be blessed. Have no fear of them, nor be troubled, ¹⁵ but in your hearts honor Christ the Lord as holy, always being prepared to make a defense to anyone who asks you for a reason for the hope that is in you; yet do it with gentleness and respect, ¹⁶ having a good conscience, so that, when you are slandered, those who revile your good behavior in Christ may be put to shame. ¹⁷ For it is better to suffer for doing good, if that should be God›s will, than for doing evil.

As seen in the previous pericopal examinations, the intent of this writing project is to perform an exegetical analysis of the Scriptures that provide observations associated with the life of Philip who would become known as the evangelist (Acts 21:8). Luke's description of Philip in Acts 21:8 maintains the annotation that Philip was one of the seven. Along with Philip, Stephen was Luke's inspired choice for providing a more extensive biography of the seven.[135]

The previous chapter examined the character of Stephen. This chapter will be dedicated to examining the speech of Stephen provided in Acts 7:1-53. Rather than citing all fifty-three verses in the heading of this chapter, the pericope provided is indicative of the characteristics found in Stephen's speech as he stood to make his defense before the council (Acts 6:15). A speech given after false accusations were made against Stephen, but a speech that maintained gentleness and respect (1 Peter 3:15).

Dale A. Meyer quotes that reality needs to be interpreted theologically.[136] An exegetical analysis of the speech of Stephen provides a theological interpretation of how to answer false accusers with gentleness and respect to aid in the fulfillment of God's responsive purposes.

Stephen begins by addressing the council as brothers and fathers (Acts 7:2). Robin G. Thompson identifies the council as the great Sanhedrin council.[137] The Sanhedrin was considered the highest religious court that a Jew could face; comprised of well-honored, educated,

---

[135] Charles Harris Nash, "Stephen, the Model Layman: The Unique, Transcendent Image of Jesus in Life and Death, 'Filled with all the Fulness of God.' Acts 6-7," *Review & Expositor* 23, no. 4 (Oct 1926): 452, accessed September 15, 2020, ATLA Religion Database with ATLASerials, EBSCOhost.

[136] Dale A. Meyer, "Why Go to Church Every Sunday? Three Reasons from 1 Peter," *Concordia Journal* 45, no. 1 (Wint 2019): 9, accessed October 27, 2020, ATLA Religion Database with ATLASerials, EBSCOhost.

[137] Robin G. Thompson, "Diaspora Jewish Freedmen: Stephen's Deadly Opponents," *Bibliotheca sacra* 173, no. 690 (Apr – Jun 2016): 166, accessed October 28, 2020, ATLA Religion Database with ATLASerials, EBSCOhost.

and powerful men.[138] Because these men were well-honored men among the Jewish people, Stephen addressed them in an honorable way in spite of the circumstances that brought him before them. As followers of Jesus Christ, our response to those who are considered esteemed among us should always be in an honorable way regardless of the circumstances that might bring us into their presence.

Interestingly, this is the same type of response that was demonstrated by the Apostle Paul as he stood before a hostile mob (Acts 21:27-22:1). What makes this so interesting is that scholars believe in the possibility of Paul's presence during Stephen's speech making Paul Luke's source for acquiring the details of the speech.[139] If there is some truth to these assumptions, then it would appear that not only was Paul influenced by the words of Stephen, but Paul may have also been influenced by Stephen's response seeing that he responded in like fashion. Our responses to hostility should imitate those who respond with gentleness and respect.

Romans 13:1-7 commands that we should give honor to whom honor is owed. James B. Prothro aligns recognitions of honor with the Christian duty to live peaceably with all even in the context of potentially abusive situations.[140] This type of honorable response aligns with the Apostle Peter's mandate to seek peace and pursue it even in the context of evil and reviling (1 Peter 3:11). Responding with recognitions of honor is the Christ follower's obedient attempt at actively seeking peace and pursuing it.

After honorably acknowledging the council, Stephen identifies God as the God of glory (Acts 7:2). Stephen's intent was not to ambiguously

---

[138] David Guzik, "Acts 6 – The Appointment of Deacons and the Arrest of Stephen," Enduringword.com, https://enduringword.com/bible-commentary/acts-6/.

[139] Ben Witherington III, New Testament Rhetoric: An Introductory Guide to the Art of Persuasion in and of the New Testament (Eugene, OR: Cascade Books, 2009), 59.

[140] James B. Prothro, "Distance, Tolerance, and Honor: Six Theses on Romans 13:1-7," *Concordia Journal* 42, no. 4 (Fall 2016): 294, accessed October 30, 2020, ATLA Religion Database with ATLASerials, EBSCOhost.

make reference to just any god, but to specifically make reference to the God who sits on the throne in heaven; the God whom Stephen also explicitly references in Acts 7:49 which is quoted from Isaiah 66:1.[141] God also explicitly identifies Himself as the God of Abraham, Isaac, and Jacob (Acts 7:32). As followers of Jesus Christ, our referential responses should be free from all ambiguity when we make mention of the God whom we say we serve.

Jesus Christ Himself provided the pattern for being explicit when making reference to God. In the model prayer, Jesus teaches that we should pray to the Father "who is in heaven" and it is the "heavenly" Father who is willing to forgive our trespasses (Matthew 6:9, 14). In Matthew 11:25, Jesus gives thanks to the Father "who is Lord of heaven and earth." As followers of Jesus Christ, we should especially respond to those who challenge what we believe by being explicit when making reference to God. David Seal conveys that explicitness in our expressions about God strengthens what has already been established and places God in His proper place of prominence.[142] Since the God of glory is the reason for the hope that is within us (1 Peter 3:15), then we should be explicit when making reference to Him.

Stephen's identification of God as the God of glory may be an allusion to Psalm 29. The Psalmist writes that the Lord should be ascribed the glory that is due His name. A large number of scholars believe Psalm 29 to be an adaptation of an older Canaanite hymn to the storm-god

---

[141.] Aaron W. White, "The Apostolic Preaching of the Lord Jesus: Seeing the Speeches in Acts as a Coherent Series of Sermons," *Presbyterion* 44, no. 2 (Fall 2018): 42, accessed November 11, 2020, ATLA Religion Database with ATLASerials, EBSCOhost.

[142.] David Seal, "The Lord's Prayer Prayed," *Restoration Quarterly* 61, no. 2 (2019): 79-80, accessed November 12, 2020, ATLA Religion Database with ATLASerials, EBSCOhost.

Baal.[143] In the Ugaritic religious worldview, the storm-god Baal is considered to be a second-tier deity that is in conflict with the chaotic sea god Yamm.[144]

The adaptation of Psalm 29 insists that glory and honor only belong to the God whose voice thunders over the waters and is enthroned over the flood (Psalm 29:3,10). He is more than just a god of the seas and the storm; He is the God who is over the seas and storm. Removing all ambiguity when making reference to the God of heaven adds the same insistence that only glory and honor belong to Him.

The bulk of the content of Stephen's response to those who reviled him was a recollection of the history of God's interactions with His chosen people. Michael Patella labels the historical aspects of Stephen's response as the recitation of the story of salvation's history.[145] A history that is outlined by Earl J. Richard as the History of the Patriarchs (Acts 7:2-16), the History of Moses (Acts 7:17:34), and the Thematic Section (Acts 7:35-50).[146] The Thematic Section being a reference to the theme of Hebrew rejection and rebellion against God.[147] Stephen's response through Acts 7:50 is replete with a historical understanding of God's

---

[143] Joseph I. Hunt, "Translating Psalm 29: Towards a Commentary on the Psalms of the 1979 Book of Common Prayer," Anglican Theological Review 67, no. 3 (Jul 1985): 222, accessed November 11, 2020, ATLA Religion Database with ATLASerials, EBSCOhost.

[144] Ryan S. Higgins, "The Good, the God, and the Ugly: The Role of the Beloved Monster in the Ancient Near East and the Hebrew Bible," Interpretation 74, no. 2 (Apr 2020): 135, accessed November 27, 2020, ATLA Religion Database with ATLASerials, EBSCOhost.

[145] Michael Patella, "Do Not Hold This Sin Against Them – The Martyrdom of Stephen (Acts 7)," The Bible Today 55, no. 3 (May-Jun 2017): 198-199, accessed November 18, 2020, ATLA Religion Database with ATLASerials, EBSCOhost.

[146] Earl J. Richard, "The Polemical Character of the Joseph Episode in Acts 7," Journal of Biblical Literature 98, no. 2 (Jun 1979): 257, accessed November 18, 2020, ATLA Religion Database with ATLASerials, EBSCOhost.

[147] J. Julius Scott, Jr., "Stephen's Speech: A Possible Model for Luke's Historical Method," Journal of the Evangelical Theological Society 17, no. 2 (Spr 1974): 93, accessed November 18, 2020, ATLA Religion Database with ATLASerials, EBSCOhost.

dealings with His chosen people. As followers of Jesus Christ, who are now considered to be among God's chosen people (1 Peter 2:9-10), we should have a historical understanding of how God has dealt with His people because it informs us how God will faithfully deal with us. Scott rightly stated that Stephen's speech should be considered more apologetic than evangelistic especially since his speech was also a defense for the hope that was within him.[148] The hope that is within us is strengthened by our understanding of how God has historically dealt with His people and our defense for that hope is found in our history.

Romans 15:4 teaches that it is through the endurance and the encouragement of the Scriptures that we have hope which is why we are to be instructed by them. Benjamin Mayes suggests that the word of God is paracletic in its application.[149] The word of God comes alongside of us to give comfort and hope.

For the followers of Jesus Christ, the Scriptures are also our history book. The instructions that we receive from them give us comfort and hope which is why the knowledge of that history is a defense for the hope that lies within us. Therefore, we should be able to respond historically to those who ask us for the reason for the hope that lies within us.

Embedded in the historicity of Stephen's speech is the acknowledgement of the fulfillment of prophecy. Stephen makes reference to the fulfillment of Canaanite territories being given to Abraham's offspring for a possession (7:3-5, 44-45), the fulfillment of the Israelite Egyptian enslavement and their deliverance from it (Acts 7:6-7, 35-36), and most importantly the fulfillment of raising up a prophet after the model of Moses who is identified as the Righteous One (Acts 7: 37, 52). Ju-Won Kim believes that Luke's intent through these references is to demonstrate how the promise given to Abraham led up to the ultimate

---

[148] Ibid., 91.

[149] Benjamin T G Mayes, "The Useful Application of Scripture in Lutheran Orthodoxy: An Aid to Contemporary Preaching and Exegesis," *Concordia Theology Quarterly* 83, no. 1-2 (Jan-Apr 2019): 128, accessed November 23, 2020, ATLA Religion Database with ATLASerials, EBSCOhost.

fulfillment of the coming of the Christ.[150] A defense for the hope that lies within us is God's ability to fulfill all that has been prophesied and promised to us by Him. Prophetic fulfillments of the past should produce an unwavering confidence that God is able to fulfill prophecies that have not yet come to pass.

God Himself declared that with the same power with which He caused the former things to come to pass, He can also cause the new things that He declares to spring forth (Isaiah 42:9). Prophetic fulfillments are confirmations of God's incomparable power and provide the confidence that prophecies that are yet to be accomplished will also be done through His direction, through His power, and under His guidance.[151]

Jesus Christ, the revelation of God in the flesh (John 1:1, 14), in like fashion prophesied of Judas' betrayal (John 13). Jesus proclaimed to His disciples that what He was telling them about the betrayal, He was telling them before it took place so that when it took place, they would believe in Him (John 13:19). Ellicott's Commentary states that the declaration of Judas' betrayal prior to the event was intended to provide confirmation of the disciples' faith in Jesus as the Messiah.[152] The hope that lies within us in Jesus as the Messiah should also be confirmed by His ability to pre-declare fulfilled prophetic events especially the fulfillment of the events associated with Judas' betrayal.

In association with the prophecy of Judas' betrayal, Jesus quotes Psalm 41:9, "He who ate my bread has lifted his heel against me." Jesus expresses that Judas' election was for the purpose of this Scripture being fulfilled (John 13:18). In Pesher interpretive-like fashion, Jesus

---

[150] Ju-Won Kim, "Explicit Quotations from Genesis Within the Context of Stephen's Speech in Acts," *Neotestamentica* 41, no. 2 (2007): 355, accessed November 24, 2020, ATLA Religion Database with ATLASerials, EBSCOhost.

[151] Celiane Vieira, "Isaiah 42: The Mission of the Servant," *Missio apostolica* 22, no. 1 (May 2014): 131, 133, accessed November 25, 2020, ATLA Religion Database with ATLASerials, EBSCOhost.

[152] "Ellicott's Commentary for English Readers," Bible Hub, accessed November 29, 2020, https://biblehub.com/commentaries/ellicott/john/13.htm.

was describing that "this is that" which was spoken of in Psalm 41:9 and that it was by His hand that the Scripture was being fulfilled which is why He stated I know whom I have chosen.[153] Jesus' election of Judas for the purpose of fulfilling Psalm 41:9 provides an additional defense that Jesus truly is the radiance of the glory of God and the exact imprint of His nature (Hebrews 1:3) being also able to cause former things to come to pass. This should instill in us a confidence in His ability to fulfill prophecies yet to come, strengthening the hope that lies within us.

Johnathan Pritchett believes that Old Testament quotations by New Testament authors carries the intent of opening our minds to the larger context.[154] The context of Psalm 41 not only provides the prophecy of Judas' betrayal, but it also alludes to the vindication of Christ (Psalm 41:10-12); described by N.T. Wright as also being the vindication for all those who believe in Him.[155] There is no greater prophetic fulfillment than Jesus Christ being risen from the grave. This is the true power for the hope that lies within us especially in the hope that we have in the promised life beyond the grave.

Also, within the historicity of Stephen's speech there are two relational representations; those, who for the most part, obeyed God and those who acted contrary. Those, who for the most part, obeyed God are identified as Abraham, Isaac, Jacob, Joseph, Moses, Joshua, David, and Solomon. Those who acted contrary are identified as the patriarchs who acted out of jealousy (Acts 7:9) and the fathers who refused to obey (Acts 7:39). Richard labels these strands of Hebrew history as bitter and negative, the part of Hebrew history that Christianity should

---

[153] G. K. Beale, ed., *The Right Doctrine from the Wrong Texts? Essays on the Use of the Old Testament in the New*, (Grand Rapids: Baker Academics 1994), part 1, Kindle.

[154] Johnathan Pritchett, "New Testament Use of the Old Testament," (lecture, Trinity College of the Bible and Theological Seminary, Evansville, IN).

[155] N. T. Wright, *The Resurrection Son of God: Christian Origins and the Question of God, Volume 3*, (London: Fortress Press, 2003), section 5.7(ii), Kindle.

reject.[156] Stephen associates his listeners with those who acted contrary. He described them as being stiff-necked, uncircumcised in heart and ears, always resisting the Holy Spirit (Acts 7:51); words of rebuke that were inspired by Scripture (e.g., Exodus 32:9).

Though Stephen's response to the Sanhedrin council was offered with gentleness and respect, Stephen was also blatantly honest with them especially as it related to their contrariness. When responding to those who seek an answer for the reason for the hope that lies within us, the followers of Jesus Christ should be unafraid and unashamed to be blatantly honest about behavior that is contrary to God's will.

The sacred writings of Scripture are identified as being profitable for reproof (2 Timothy 3:16). Edward W. Goodrick stresses that Scripture forms the words of reproof to those who should know better.[157] Stephen most assuredly emphasizes this when he reminds his Jewish listeners that they were the ones who received the law as delivered by angels and yet, they did not keep it (Acts 7:53). They should have known better. When the follower of Jesus Christ encounters those whose behavior is found to be contrary to the will of God, in particular the behavior of those who claim to be followers of Jesus Christ, then reproof is both necessary and appropriate. But just as Stephens words of rebuke were inspired by the Scriptures, our words of rebuke should be inspired by them as well. Only God's word identifies what is sin and only God's word should be used as words of rebuke; but even our words of rebuke should be exercised with both gentleness and respect (Galatians 6:1).

In summation, Stephen's speech is representative of how God would have us to respond to false accusers as we make a defense for the reason for the hope that lies within us. The followers of Jesus Christ should always respond with respectability, especially towards those who hold

---

[156] Richard, 264.

[157] Edward W. Goodrick, "Let's Put 2 Timothy 3:16 Back in the Bible," Journal of the Evangelical Theological Society 25, no. 4 (Dec 1982): 485, accessed December 9, 2020, ATLA Religion Database with ATLASerials, EBSCOhost.

positions of honor. Our honorable responses are a testimony of true Christian behavior even in the face of abusive situations.

Any referential responses made to the God whom we serve should be explicit so that there will be no confusion to anything else that might be considered a god to someone else. The follower of Jesus Christ should make clear and definite distinctions to the God who sits in heaven, who gave His only begotten Son as a sacrifice for our sins.

The follower of Jesus Christ should be historically astute. The defense for the hope that lies within us is found in how the God of heaven has historically dealt with His people because it defines how God will faithfully deal with all those who have bowed the knee to Jesus Christ.

Prophetic fulfillments add strength to our hope. Only the God of heaven, which is also the God who allowed Himself to become flesh, can declare what will come to pass and cause them to be fulfilled by His own hand.

Though gentleness and respect should be the highlight of our responses, honesty with those who are contrary should also be included especially with those who are followers of the faith. Honesty with those who are contrary should come with the heart-felt intent of helping them to find their way back (Matthew 18:15).

CHAPTER SIX
Fulfilling God's Contrasting Purposes

Acts 7:54-60 (ESV)

⁵⁴ Now when they heard these things they were enraged, and they ground their teeth at him. ⁵⁵ But he, full of the Holy Spirit, gazed into heaven and saw the glory of God, and Jesus standing at the right hand of God. ⁵⁶ And he said, "Behold, I see the heavens opened, and the Son of Man standing at the right hand of God." ⁵⁷ But they cried out with a loud voice and stopped their ears and rushed together at him. ⁵⁸ Then they cast him out of the city and stoned him. And the witnesses laid down their garments at the feet of a young man named Saul. ⁵⁹ And as they were stoning Stephen, he called out, "Lord Jesus, receive my spirit." ⁶⁰ And falling to his knees he cried out with a loud voice, "Lord, do not hold this sin against them." And when he had said this, he fell asleep.

Jesus Christ specifically warns that reactions to the answers that we provide for the hope that lies within us will not always be received in a favorable fashion. Jesus Himself said that negative reactions can be as extensive as betrayal, hatred, and for some even death. These negative reactions will occur because of His name's sake (Luke 21:16-17).

The Pulpit Commentary labels these negative reactions as the price of friendship with Jesus Christ.[158] No matter how good our intentions may be, the God-given speech and wisdom with which we use as a defense to respond to those who oppose us (Luke 21: 14-15) has the possibility of being met with hostility. Steven Nation insists that nobody who is a faithful defender of the faith will escape at least some degree of opposition.[159]

Stephen's speech engendered rage and the grinding of teeth. David H. Wenkel considers the grinding of teeth to be an outward demonstration of rage.[160] The rage directed at Stephen was far from being a rage that was internalized. One might say that it was written all over their faces.

The focus for the follower of Jesus Christ should not be the rage that was directed toward Stephen, but the contrasting reaction of Stephen. The purpose to be fulfilled by the follower of Jesus Christ is to have a contrasting reaction towards those who strike out in hostility at them. Merriam-Webster defines the verb form of the word contrast as to compare or appraise in respect to difference.[161] When an appraisal is made of how the follower of Jesus Christ reacts to hostile responses toward verbalizations of faith, there ought to be a distinct difference as opposed to those who are not followers of Christ.

After being nailed to a cross, insulted, and abused, Jesus Christ said, "Father, forgive them, for they know not what they do" (Luke 23:34); a reaction that was in complete contrast to what was being done and

---

[158] "Pulpit Commentary," Bible Hub, accessed December 22, 2020, https://biblehub.com/commentaries/pulpit/luke/21.htm.

[159] Steven Nation, "Martyr in Every Sense of the Word: Learning from the Life and Death of Stephen, the First Known Martyr," Churchman 125, no. 2 (Sum 2011): 176, accessed January 10, 2021, ATLA Religion Database with ATLASerials, EBSCOhost.

[160] David H. Wenkel, "The Gnashing of Teeth of Jesus' Opponents," Bibliotheca sacra 175, no. 697 (Jan–Mar 2018): 83, accessed December 23, 2020, ATLA Religion Database with ATLASerials, EBSCOhost.

[161] Merriam-Webster, Webster's Ninth New Collegiate College Dictionary (Springfield, MA: Merriam-Webster, Inc., 1985).

directed toward Him. Piotr Nyk insists that the same radicalism that was exhibited in the life of Christ should also be resembled in the life of His disciples.[162] Stephen was imaging the same contrasting reaction that was demonstrated in the life of Jesus Christ; the same contrasting reaction that should also be emulated in the lives of all those who refer to themselves as followers of Jesus Christ.

Luke attributes Stephen's contrasting reaction to being full of the Holy Spirit. Within a short span of two chapters (Acts 6, 7), Stephen is twice described as being full of the Holy Spirit. Not only was he specifically described as being full of the Holy Spirit, but Luke also makes it clear that this was a characteristic that was easily identifiable since this was one of the characteristics that resulted in Stephen being chosen as one of the seven. It would not be a stretch to conclude that being full of the Holy Spirit was a constant in the life of Stephen and it was this constant that caused him to react in a contrasting fashion. Ellicott's Commentary for English Readers states that being full of the Holy Spirit was not a sudden inspiration but a description of Stephen's permanent state.[163] As followers of Jesus Christ, being full of the Holy Spirit should be a constant in our lives and this constant will be the instigator of our contrasting reactions to hostility.

Ephesians 5:15-18 describes being filled with the Spirit (the Spirit being a synonymous term for the Holy Ghost) as a carefully lived life according to wisdom, the wisdom that is received through the understood will of the Lord.[164] Many translations utilize the word "walk" as opposed to the word "live" and is intended as a metaphorical reference

---

[162] Piotr Nyk, "You are Witnesses of These Things! (Luke 24:48): The Concept of Testimony in the Gospel of Luke," *Verbum Vitae* 27, (2015): 121, accessed December 23, 2020, ATLA Religion Database with ATLASerials, EBSCOhost.

[163] "Ellicott's Commentary for English Readers," Bible Hub, accessed December 29, 2020, https://biblehub.com/commentaries/ellicott/acts/7.htm.

[164] Len Woods, *Understanding the Holy Spirit Made Easy*, (Peabody, MA: Rose Publishing, LLC, 2018), 9.

to a continued mode of conduct or behavior.[165] As followers of Jesus Christ, living life according to the will of the Lord should not be a sporadic event, but how life is lived continuously. A life lived continuously according to the will of God is a life that is constantly filled with the Holy Spirit especially since it is the Holy Spirit who leads and guides us according to God's will. When life is lived continuously according to the will of God, then God's contrasting purposes will be fulfilled.

The imperative provided in Scripture to be full of the Holy Spirit is situated rhetorically in a context that is replete with contrasts.[166] A sampling of those contrasts include once being dead in trespasses and sin, but now being made alive together with Christ (Ephesians 2:5), once following the course of this world, but now walking according to the good works that God prepared beforehand (Ephesians 2:1, 10), once being far off and separated from Christ, but now brought near by the blood of Christ (Ephesians 2:11-13), putting off the old self which belongs to our former manner of life and putting on the new self which is created after the likeness of God (Ephesians 4:22-24), and no longer partnering with those who walk in darkness, but now walking with the children of light (Ephesians 5:7-8). Timothy G. Gombis defines these contrasts as the life that characterizes the followers of Christ.[167] The Apostle Paul's very intention in the book of Ephesians is to identify the followers of Jesus Christ as a contrast to those who do not follow Him. If the follower of Jesus Christ is identified as a contrast to those who do not, then their reactions to hostility should match their identity.

---

[165]. Wesley L. Gerig, "Walk," Biblestudytools.com, accessed January 12, 2021, https://www.biblestudytools.com/dictionary/walk/.

[166]. Timothy G. Gombis, "Being the Fullness of God in Christ by the Spirit: Ephesians 5:18 in its Epistolary Setting," *Tyndale Bulletin* 53, no. 2 (2002): 265, accessed January 10, 2021, ATLA Religion Database with ATLASerials, EBSCOhost.

[167]. Ibid.

Though teeth were being ground at Stephen, Stephen did not grind his teeth in return. Stephen maintained his focus on heaven. The chapter pericope emphasizes that Stephen gazed into heaven. If the follower of Jesus Christ is to exhibit a contrasting reaction towards hostility directed toward them, then the focus must not be on the behavior of the hostiles, the maintained focus must be on heaven.

The letter to the Colossian saints and the faithful in Christ encouraged them to have a set mind (a metaphor for having a fixed gaze or focus) on the things above where Christ is seated at the right hand of God and not on earthly things (Colossians 3:1-2).[168] The same contrasting reaction that was imaged by Stephen was also prescribed to the Colossian saints and the faithful in Christ. If the followers of Jesus Christ endeavor to fulfill the contrasting purposes of God, then they must also maintain a fixed gaze and a set mind on the things above where Christ is seated at the right hand of God and not on earthly things. Earthly things contextually being a reference to the doctrines, traditions, and behaviors of those who live ungodly (Colossians 2).

It is worth noting that Saul who would become known as the Apostle Paul (disputedly credited with authoring the letter to the Colossians) was a witness to the contrasting reaction of Stephen (Acts 7:58).[169] Disputers might have to consider as one of the arguments for Pauline authorship of Colossians that Stephen's contrasting reaction may have influenced what the Apostle Paul prescribed to the Colossian saints.

Luke details that Stephen's gaze into heaven caused him to see the glory of God. The psalmist declared that it is quite difficult to gaze into heaven and not see the glory of God because the heavens

---

[168]. "G816 – atenizō–Outline of Biblical Usage," Blue Letter Bible, accessed January 19, 2021, https://www.blueletterbible.org/lang/lexicon/lexicon.cfm?Strongs=G816&t=ESV.

[169]. Amanda C. Miller, "Paul's Social Network in Colossians: Friends and Coworkers in the Lycus Valley," Review & Expositor 116, no. 4 (Nov 2019): 437, accessed January 19, 2021, ATLA Religion Database with ATLASerials, EBSCOhost.

declare God's glory and the sky above proclaims His handiwork (Psalm 19:1). William P. Brown refers to Psalm 19 as the communicator of God's glory.[170]

The writer of Hebrews declares that Jesus is the radiance of the glory of God (Hebrews 1:3). Kenneth L. Schenck believes this declaration to be among the most important exaltation texts in the whole of the New Testament.[171] Therefore in this instance, one might argue that the glory that Stephen saw was Jesus standing at the right hand of God. Being full of the Holy Spirit, Stephen was enabled to see beyond those things that were physical (i.e., the hostility that was being directed toward him) because his intentional focus was upon that which is spiritual (Jesus standing at the right hand of God) empowering him to react in a contrasting deportment. The image of Jesus standing was probably a reminder to Stephen that he should also stand in the same contrasting manner as Jesus stood before those who directed hostilities toward Him, with the power of God on His side. When Christ followers intentionally focus on that which is spiritual (e.g., that which enables us to stand against the schemes of the devil– Ephesians 6:10-18), then they are enabled to see beyond the hostilities that are directed toward them and are empowered to fulfill God's contrasting purposes because they have the power of God on their side.

Ephesians 6:12 provides the edification that we do not wrestle against flesh and blood but against the rulers, against the authorities, against the cosmic powers over this present darkness, against the spiritual forces of evil in the heavenly places; described by Paul T. Eckel as the four antagonists with whom the Christian must do battle.[172]

[170.] William P. Brown, "The Joy of Lex and the Language of Glory in Psalm 19," Journal for Preachers 43, no. 4 (Pentecost 2020): 12-13, accessed January 20, 2021, ATLA Religion Database with ATLASerials, EBSCOhost.

[171.] Kenneth L. Schenck, "A Celebration of the Enthroned Son: The Catena of Hebrews 1," *Journal of Biblical Literature* 120, no. 3 (Fall 2001): 472, accessed January 20, 2021, ATLA Religion Database with ATLASerials, EBSCOhost.

[172.] Paul T. Eckel, "Ephesians 6:10-20," Interpretation 45, no. 3 (Jul 1991): 289, accessed January 20, 2021, ATLA Religion Database with ATLASerials, EBSCOhost.

Unless the hostilities directed toward the followers of Jesus Christ are properly identified as spiritual rather than carnal, then fulfilling God's contrasting purposes will be difficult because the reaction will more than likely conform to the hostiles as opposed to conforming to the Christ.[173] Christ followers revenge disobedience when their obedience is fulfilled (2 Corinthians 10:6). Obedience is fulfilled by responding to hostility in the same contrasting fashion as was demonstrated by Christ.

Even though hostilities were being directed at Stephen, he was still willing to share the revelation that was shared with him. Stephen said, "Behold, I see the heavens opened and the Son of Man standing at the right hand of God." Fulfillment of the contrasting purposes of God also means being willing to share revelations from God even though hostilities are directed toward us.

In responding to the question of when the temple would be destroyed, Jesus remarked that prior to its destruction persecutions would come, but as disciples of Jesus Christ they were to view persecutions as an opportunity to be a witness (Luke 21:5-19). Walter Brueggemann refers to the times of persecution as the times of expectation, the times when we are expected to share the truths of God that have been entrusted to us.[174] To be able to fulfill the contrasting purposes of God, the follower of Jesus Christ must have a broader perspective of the times of persecution. The times of persecution should also be viewed as an opportunity to be a witness; an opportunity to share the revelations of God.

Stephen's willingness to share the revelation that he received from God was met with increased hostilities. The whole gathering demonstrated a refusal to hear the revelation that Stephen was sharing with them; they stopped their ears, they rushed upon him, cast him out

---

[173] Ibid., 290.

[174] Walter Brueggemann, "On Appearing Before the Authorities," *Journal for Preachers* 36, no. 4 (Pentecost 2013): 22-23, accessed January 24, 2021, ATLA Religion Database with ATLASerials, EBSCOhost.

of the city, and proceeded to stone him. The most disappointing element of the hostile reactions toward Stephen was the refusal of the so-called men of God to listen to the revelation that was being shared with them. For the follower of Jesus Christ, the most disappointing element associated with times of persecution will not be the who of those who persecute them, but the unwillingness to hear the revelations that have come from God. David Guzik describes this type of reaction as spiritual insanity, an indication of having religion apart from having a real relationship with Jesus Christ.[175]

Jesus Christ Himself said that this type of behavior is indicative of those who do not know the Father or Him, disappointingly even those who are considered to be members of the religious community (John 16:1-4); a hostility from within as opposed to coming from without.[176] This prophetic utterance of Christ should remove surprise though disappointment may remain, especially with those whom we would expect to demonstrate a more receptive reaction to the shared revelations that have come from God.

Luke emphasizes that the contrasting reactions of Stephen continued to occur during the crescendo of the hostility, as they were stoning him. The real proof of a mature follower of Jesus Christ is when contrasting reactions continue to be exuded even after hostilities have reached their peak. The brother of Jesus, to whom the book of James is traditionally attributed, referred to this characteristic as remaining steadfast under trial as a demonstration of one's love for God (James 1:12).[177] J. Ronald Blue believes that steadfastness under

---

[175] David Guzik, "Study Guide for Acts 7," Blue Letter Bible, accessed January 27, 2021, https://www.blueletterbible.org/Comm/guzik_david/StudyGuide2017-Act/Act-7.cfm?a=1025057.

[176] Kari Syreeni, "Partial Weaning: Approaching the Psychological Enigma of John 13-17," *Svensk Exegetisk Arsbok* 72, (2007): 183, accessed January 29, 2021, ATLA Religion Database with ATLASerials, EBSCOhost.

[177] J. Ronald Blue, Bible Knowledge Commentary: An Exposition of the Scriptures by Dallas Seminary Faculty: New Testament Edition, ed. John F. Walvoord and Roy B. Zuck (Colorado Springs: ChariotVictor Publishing, 1983), 815.

trial is the revelation of a love for God and it is the love for God that enables believers to remain steadfast.[178] Continuing to exude contrasting reactions even after hostilities have reached their peak provides the evidence of a love for God.

It would be negligent to close this chapter on Stephen's life without specifying that in the midst of this horrific event, Stephen openly acknowledged Jesus as Lord. For those of us who are seeking to fulfill the contrasting purposes of God, there is no greater way to glorify God than to acknowledge the Lordship of Jesus Christ in the midst of increased hostilities.

Each time the word Lord is used in this pericope, it makes reference to Jesus as being supreme in all authority.[179] Charles T. P. Grierson declares that this is the highest confession of His Person.[180] Stephen was openly acknowledging that Jesus had the authority to receive his spirit and the authority to not hold this sin against them; both being acknowledgements that Jesus is God (Ecclesiastes 12:7, Isaiah 43:25). In the midst of increased hostilities there is no greater contrasting reaction than to openly acknowledge Jesus as Lord and to acknowledge His authority as God.

In summary, God does not expect the follower of Jesus Christ to return evil for evil when hostilities are directed toward them (1 Peter 3:9). God expects for His children to have a reaction that contrasts hostilities. When appraisals are made about the behavior of those who intentionally or unintentionally find themselves in hostile situations, the behavior of those who follow Christ should be reported as vastly different than the hostile aggressors. The constant and consistent

---

[178] Ibid.

[179] "G2962 – kyrios – Strong's Definitions / Concordance Results Using ESV," Blue Letter Bible, accessed February 3, 2021, https://www.blueletterbible.org/lang/lexicon/lexicon.cfm?page=6&strongs=G2962&t=ESV#lexResults.

[180] Charles T.P. Grierson, *Hastings Dictionary of the Bible (4 Volumes in One): A Dictionary of the Bible*, ed. James Hastings, D.D. (Harrington, DE: Delmarva Publications), Kindle.

passion to live according to the will of God should override any urges to parallel or to return hostilities. As followers of Jesus Christ, our focus should be on emulating the contrasting behaviors of Christ and not on those who direct hostilities toward us.

The opportunity to share the revelations of God should always be a priority during hostile engagements. Hostilities encountered should be considered as an opportunity to glorify God by sharing the revelations of God. There is no greater revelation to share with hostile aggressors than to openly acknowledge the Lordship of Christ and to acknowledge His authority as God.

CHAPTER SEVEN
FULFILLING GOD'S SCATTERATION PURPOSES

Acts 8:1-4 (ESV)

¹ And Saul approved of his execution. And there arose on that day a great persecution against the church in Jerusalem, and they were all scattered throughout the regions of Judea and Samaria, except the apostles. ² Devout men buried Stephen and made great lamentation over him. ³ But Saul was ravaging the church, and entering house after house, he dragged off men and women and committed them to prison. ⁴ Now those who were scattered went about preaching the word.

As noted in the previous chapter, persecution in the lives of the followers of Jesus Christ serves a purpose. That purpose is to provide opportunities to be a witness for Christ. Reiterated from Walter Brueggemann, the times of persecution are a time when we are expected to share the truths of God that have been entrusted to us.[181] The followers of Jesus Christ possess "the truth," the word that has been given to us by God Himself (John 17:17). God's expectation for His

---

[181.] Walter Brueggemann, "On Appearing Before the Authorities," *Journal for Preachers* 36, no. 4 (Pentecost 2013): 22-23, accessed January 24, 2021, ATLA Religion Database with ATLASerials, EBSCOhost.

followers is to be worldwide sharers of the truth. The pericope for this chapter provides that the times of persecution can be adopted by God as a prodder and a motivator; motivation for the children of God to obey what He has commanded, the commandment to be teachers of all that He has commanded to all nations.

The commanded mission for the church as delineated to the eleven disciples was to make disciples of all nations, baptizing them in the name of the Father and of the Son and of the Holy Spirit, teaching them to observe all that Christ has commanded; to go with full confidence that the resurrected Christ (aka, the conqueror of death), the one who has all authority in heaven and on earth would be with them (Matthew 28:16-20).

The commanded mission of the church is traditionally known as the Great Commission, but is affectionately referred to by Walter Klaiber as the Great Assurance.[182] The assurance provided by Christ because of His unlimited authority and the assurance of His continuing presence, He promised that He would be with them always to the end of the age.[183] A promise that is hermeneutically extended to every follower of Jesus Christ considering that the first disciples would not live physically or bodily until the end of the age.[184] The end of the age being defined by John Peter Lange as the end of this aeon; when all corruption has past and immortality has truly begun.[185] The Great Commission tasks every follower of Jesus Christ to fulfill the scatteration purpose, to be teachers of all that God has commanded to all nations.

---

[182] Walter Klaiber, "The Great Commission of Matthew 28:16-20," *American Baptist Quarterly* 37, no.2 (Sum 2018): 110, accessed February 10, 2021, ATLA Religion Database with ATLASerials, EBSCOhost.

[183] Ibid.

[184] Kolawole Olumafemi Paul, "The Great Commission Mandate of the Church in Matthew 28:18-20," *Word & World* 40, no. 4 (Fall 2020): 424, accessed February 17, 2021, ATLA Religion Database with ATLASerials, EBSCOhost.

[185] John Peter Lange, "Lange Commentary on the Holy Scriptures," Bible Hub, accessed February 21, 2021, https://biblehub.com/commentaries/lange/matthew/13.htm.

The Greek parsing of the "go" imperative of the Great Commission is provided in the aorist tense, a tense which has no regard for time.[186] This implies that there should not be a time when the follower of Christ does not feel compelled to teach all nations all that Christ has commanded. This includes that there should be no prejudice or hesitation as it relates to the who or the topic of discussion. It does not matter who the conversation is with or the topic being discussed, what God has commanded should find its way into the discussion as the opportunity presents itself.

The Apostle Paul refers to this effort as a wide door of opportunity for an effectual work to be done (1 Corinthians 16:9). Johann Bengel expresses that it should be the part of a wise man to watch for such opportunities.[187] Anytime a topic is being discussed which relates to some theme which is found in Scripture, then the follower of Jesus Christ should always be willing to walk through such wide doors of opportunity and share what God has said about the matter at hand. If time or prejudice becomes a hindrance to teaching all that Christ has commanded to all nations, then there will be a failure in the fulfillment of God's scatteration purposes.

The general rules of hermeneutics furnish that context provides the most accurate meaning for words.[188] An interpretation must agree with the general message of the context which is derived from the nature of the words.[189] The rules of hermeneutics should help us to determine the most accurate meaning of the word "baptizing" as it is utilized in the Great Commission.

---

[186] "G4198 – poreuō – Tools," Blue Letter Bible, accessed April 7, 2021, https://www.blueletterbible.org/esv/mat/28/19/t_conc_957019.

[187] Johann Bengel, "Bengel's Gnomon of the New Testament," Bible Hub, accessed April 4, 2021, https://biblehub.com/commentaries/bengel/1_corinthians/16.htm.

[188] William W. Klein, Craig L. Blomberg, and Robert L. Hubbard, Jr., *Introduction to Biblical Interpretation*, rev. ed. (Nashville: Thomas Nelson Publishers, 2004), 215.

[189] Ibid.

The word baptizing is contextually situated between the imperative to teach. A disciple is a learner and for disciples to be made, they need to be taught. The disciples that Jesus commanded to be made are to be taught to observe all that He has commanded. Therefore, the baptizing that should take place is a baptismal in the teachings of all that Christ has commanded.

The proper definition of baptizing is to immerge or to submerge.[190] Every follower of Jesus Christ who is determined to fulfill their scatteration purposes is to immerge and to submerge all nations in the teachings of all that has been commanded by Christ. Just like a husband is commanded to cleanse his wife by the washing of water with the word (Ephesians 5:25), the followers of Christ are commanded to do the same, cleanse all nations by the washing of water with the word. Though they may return like dogs to vomit or a sow to wallow in the mud (2 Peter 2:22), the followers of Jesus Christ are only responsible for fulfilling the scatteration purposes to which they have been called.

John the Baptist made a distinct difference between his baptismal and the baptismal of Christ.[191] John the Baptist baptized with water for repentance and the baptismal of Christ is with the Holy Spirit and fire (Matthew 3:11). In the context of the Great Commission, we find a third distinction for baptismal; the baptismal which is required of every follower of Jesus Christ, the baptismal of all that Christ has commanded.

The commanded mission for the church was reiterated just prior to the ascension of Christ (Acts 1:1-11). Jesus explicitly stated that the disciples should not depart from Jerusalem until their baptism with the Holy Spirit had been fulfilled. Once their baptism with the Holy Spirit had been fulfilled, they would be endowed with the necessary power to be Christ's witnesses not only in Jerusalem, but also in Judea and Samaria, and to the end of the earth. Jesus Christ summarized His own

---

[190.] "G907 – baptizō – Thayer's Greek Lexicon," Blue Letter Bible, accessed March 11, 2021, https://www.blueletterbible.org/lang/lexicon/lexicon.cfm?Strongs=G907&t=ESV.

[191.] "G907 – baptizō – Outline of Biblical Usage," Blue Letter Bible, accessed March 11, 2021, https://www.blueletterbible.org/lang/lexicon/lexicon.cfm?Strongs=G907&t=ESV.

mission as the compulsion to bring the good news of God's reign from city to city (Luke 4:43).[192] The same mission which all Christ followers should feel compelled to fulfill, the mission of bringing the good news of God's reign from city to city; the reign which is actualized through the obedience of all that Christ has commanded, an obedience which is taught by the followers of Jesus Christ in fulfillment of God's scatteration purposes.

Acts 2 details the empowering of the disciples to be Christ's witnesses to all the nations. We are told that the day of this fulfillment was the day of Pentecost when all of the disciples were filled with the Holy Spirit, the same Spirit which indwells all who are committed followers of Jesus Christ (1 Corinthians 3:16); the same Spirit which is declared to be the one and only power necessary for the church to fulfill its mission.[193] The same Spirit that empowered the first disciples to be witnesses for Christ empowers every committed follower of Christ to be witnesses for Him. Christ's Spirit is the engine by which Christ is setting up His kingdom.[194] The same engine that should drive and empower every Christ follower to fulfill the scatteration purpose to be teachers of all that Christ has commanded.

It must not go without saying that for the follower of Christ to be able to teach all that Christ has commanded, there must be an awareness of what has been commanded. The lifelong goal of the follower of Jesus Christ should be to increase in their knowledge of Scripture. The Christ follower was not called to remain stagnant in their development as a Christian, but to grow in the knowledge of what Christ has commanded. James Burton Coffman insists that growing in knowledge is

---

[192] Celia I. Wolff, "Sharing the Gospel as Witness to Jesus: Acts 1:1-11," Word & World 39, no. 4 (Fall 2019): 374, accessed February 21, 2021, ATLA Religion Database with ATLASerials, EBSCOhost.

[193] Augustus Hopkins Strong, "The Holy Spirit: The One and Only Power in Missions," The Journal of the Evangelical Homiletics Society 7, no. 2 (Sep 2007): 78, accessed February 26, 2021, ATLA Religion Database with ATLASerials, EBSCOhost.

[194] Strong, 72.

the progression that is expected of the Christian, a progression which is achieved through diligent study.[195] The Scriptural mandate to study should not be considered as an imposition only upon those who are the leaders of formal church gatherings (2 Timothy 2:15), but an imposition upon all those who claim the name of Christ. Every follower of Jesus Christ is commanded to glorify Christ and the glorification of Christ is the fruit of growing in the knowledge of our Lord and Savior Jesus Christ (2 Peter 3:18).

The persecution described in the chapter pericope that incited the scattering of the church resulted in God's word being preached throughout Judea and Samaria. Luke distinctly describes that the ravaging of the church included both men and women; some being committed to prison, but those who were scattered went about preaching the word. Both men and women fulfilling God's scatteration purposes. The chapter pericope removes any misconceived limitations associated with preaching and provides an expanded understanding which goes beyond the pulpit and gender.

Etymologically, the word "preaching" as used in the chapter pericope refers to doing the good work of being a messenger, a messenger who is sent to make known the purposes of God.[196] Every man or woman who considers themselves to be followers of Jesus Christ should be fulfilling the purpose of being messengers who were sent to make known the purposes of God to all men. There may not be a specific call on a man or a woman to share the purposes of God in a pulpit, but there is most definitely a general call on every Christ follower to share the purposes of God out in the world. There may even be some who have misunderstood the call of God to preach in pulpits when what

---

[195] James Burton Coffman, "Bible Commentaries: Coffman Commentaries on the Bible: 2 Peter 3," Studylight.org, accessed February 28, 2021, https://www.studylight.org/commentaries/eng/bcc/2-peter-3.html.

[196] "G2097 – euangelizō – Root Word (Etymology)," Blue Letter Bible, accessed March 5, 2021, https://www.blueletterbible.org/lang/lexicon/lexicon.cfm?Strongs=G2097&t=KJV.

was really occurring was God's urging to do what He has commanded out in the world.

After declaring a blessing upon those who are persecuted for righteousness' sake, Jesus describes the persecuted as being the salt of the earth and the light of the world (Matthew 5:10 -16). The most dominant description of salt provided by the majority of commentators is its use as a preservative and a seasoning.[197] What appears to be scantily discussed is how salt is sprinkled or scattered and not simply thrown out in clumps. Just like salt is sprinkled or scattered, God has scattered His people in the earth so that they may be the light that teaches all nations to observe all that He has commanded.

Throughout Scripture, God describes Himself as the instigator for scattering His people throughout the earth particularly due to their disobedience. Deuteronomy 4 forewarns of the scattering of God's people due to idolatrous practices. Deuteronomy 28 forecasts the scattering of God's people due to disobedience of the law. Leviticus 26 provides the portent of the scattering of God's people due to contrariness toward what He had commanded. Luke even mentions in Mary's Magnificat of how God scatters the proud with the strength of His arm (Luke 1:51); described as the work of God against forces that are in opposition to His purpose.[198] Following this consistency of thought provided by Scripture, the great persecution that came against the church in Jerusalem was more than likely due to the disciples' failure to obey the commandment of Christ to be more than just witnesses in Jerusalem, but to be witnesses also in Judea and Samaria, and to the end of the earth.

---

[197] "Commentaries," BIBLETOOLS, accessed March 12, 2021, https://www.bibletools.org/index.cfm/fuseaction/Bible.show/sVerseID/23248/eVerseID/23249.

[198] Amy Smith Carman, "Ave Maria: Old Testament Allusions in the Magnificat," Priscilla Papers 31, no. 2 (Spr 2017): 16, accessed March 16, 2021, ATLA Religion Database with ATLASerials, EBSCOhost.

The etymology of the word "scattered" is compounded to denote the channel of an act through which seed might be received.[199] Since God is the instigator of the scattering of His people, the great persecution was the channel that was used by God so that the seed of His word might be received (Mark 4:14). Bertram L. Melbourne comments on how sad the church's obedience had to come under forced circumstances rather than voluntarily.[200] The preferable response for Christ followers should be an urging within themselves to teach all that Christ has commanded to all nations rather than provoking God into using such channels as persecution to entice the followers of Jesus Christ to fulfill their scatteration purposes.

Luke reports that there was an exception to the scattering of the church and that exception was the apostles. Though persecution caused the church to be scattered throughout the regions of Judea and Samaria, the apostles remained in Jerusalem. The most prescribed explanation for this exception is that Jerusalem would become the headquarters of the Christian band to which those who were scattered would refer for guidance and help.[201] Those of us who are striving to fulfill God's scatteration purposes should always have readily available to them those to whom they can refer for guidance and help.

Acts 5:42 provides an interesting association with Acts 8:3. Acts 5:42 proclaims that every day, in the temple and from house to house, they did not cease teaching and preaching that the Christ is Jesus. Acts 8:3 states that the great persecution that arose against the church in Jerusalem resulted in the ravaging of the church house after house. Rhetorically, Luke may be inferring that the teaching and the preaching

---

[199] "G1289–diaspeirō – Root Word (Etymology)," Blue Letter Bible, accessed March 16, 2021, https://www.blueletterbible.org/lang/lexicon/lexicon.cfm?Strongs=G1289&t=ESV.

[200] Bertram L. Melbourne, "Acts 1:8 Re-Examined: Is Acts 8 Its Fulfillment?" The Journal of Religious Thought 57, no. 2 (January 1, 2005): 8, accessed March 19, 2021, ATLA Religion Database with ATLASerials, EBSCOhost.

[201] J.R. Lumby, ed., *The Acts of the Apostles* (The University Press, 1888), Google Play.

that was done from house to house was the same teaching and preaching being performed by those who were scattered. In fulfillment of their scatteration purpose, what they had been taught and what had been preached to them was what those who had been scattered preached to others. This should lighten and ease the burden of those who desire to fulfill their scatteration purpose to know that what should be taught and preached are the very things that the follower of Jesus Christ has heard taught and preached to them.

When Jesus sent out the twelve Apostles, He commanded them to preach the very thing that He Himself had been preaching (Matthew 4:17, 10:5-7). Jesus also commanded them to preach those things that had been whispered to them (Matthew 10:27). The Pulpit Commentary suggests that this removes the stress upon the personality of the speaker and places the stress upon that which has been communicated.[202] Those who desire to fulfill their scatteration purposes are to preach and teach the Biblical doctrines that have been preached and taught to them. But once again it cannot go without saying that just like the Berean saints, what the follower of Jesus Christ has heard preached and taught to them should be verified by self-examination of the Scriptures (Acts 17:10-11).

In summary, as followers of Jesus Christ, we are expected to share the truths of God that have been entrusted to us. God has empowered and scattered the followers of Christ among the nations so that they might be teachers of all that Christ has commanded without prejudice and without hesitation. The call of God upon all who have committed themselves to following Christ is the fulfillment of God's scatteration purposes.

---

[202] "Pulpit Commentary," Bible Hub, accessed April 6, 2021, https://biblehub.com/commentaries/pulpit/matthew/10.htm.

CHAPTER EIGHT
FULFILLING GOD'S DISTINCTIVE PURPOSES

Acts 8:4-8 (ESV)

⁴ Now those who were scattered went about preaching the word. ⁵ Philip went down to the city of Samaria and proclaimed to them the Christ. ⁶ And the crowds with one accord paid attention to what was being said by Philip, when they heard him and saw the signs that he did. ⁷ For unclean spirits, crying out with a loud voice, came out of many who had them, and many who were paralyzed or lame were healed. ⁸ So there was much joy in that city.

As Luke begins to specifically direct our attention to Philip, Luke identifies the distinctions between Philip and the others who were scattered. The first distinction is that those who were scattered are described as those who simply "went about," no intentional or specific destination intended. But as it relates to Philip, Philip is described as having a specific destination. Philip went down to the city of Samaria. The Hebrew-Aramaic & Greek Dictionary informs us that Samaria was the name of both a city and a region in Palestine.[203] Those who were

---

[203.] Hebrew-Aramaic & Greek Dictionary, bible.lockman.org, https://bible.lockman.org/htm_php-c.php?do=show_marg_and_gh&b=44&c=8&v=5.

scattered went about the regions of Judea and Samaria (Acts 8:1), but Philip distinctly went down to the city of Samaria.

What has been established through the life of Abram, aka Abraham, is that God will provide direction to His people that seem somewhat general before He will provide direction that is very distinct and specific (Genesis 12:1, 13:14).[204] If the follower of Jesus Christ desires to receive distinctive direction from God, then they must first be willing to obey directions that seem to be somewhat general.

The second distinction between Philip and the others who were scattered is that those who were scattered went about preaching the word, but Peter went down to the city of Samaria and proclaimed to them the Christ. The author Luke intentionally uses verbiage that provides a distinction between the activity of the others who were scattered and the activity performed by Philip.

As noted in the previous chapter, etymologically the word "preaching" as used in the chapter pericope refers to doing the good work of being a messenger, a messenger who is sent to make known the purposes of God.[205] Luke provides that Philip was sharing a message that was very specific and distinct, he was proclaiming the Christ.

In the original Greek language, Luke specifically uses the word "kēryssō" to describe the activity being performed by Philip.[206] Throughout the writings of Luke, the verb "kēryssō" is utilized sixteen times and is never used in association with topics that are spoken of

---

[204.] Calvin E. Shenk, "God's Intention for Humankind: The Promise of Community: Bible Study on Genesis 12," Mission Studies 5, no. 2 (1998): 15, accessed April 27, 2021, ATLA Religion Database with ATLASerials, EBSCOhost.

[205.] "G2097 - euangelizō - Root Word (Etymology)," Blue Letter Bible, accessed March 5, 2021, https://www.blueletterbible.org/lang/lexicon/lexicon.cfm?Strongs=G2097&t=ESV.

[206.] "G2784 - kēryssō - Transliteration," Blue Letter Bible, accessed April 28, 2021, https://www.blueletterbible.org/lang/lexicon/lexicon.cfm?Strongs=G2784&t=ESV.

in a general sense.[207] The topics are always very specific. Philip was doing more than preaching about the purposes of God, Philip was proclaiming the Christ. As followers of Jesus Christ, there will be times when sharing a very general message about the purposes of God will be sufficient but there will also be times when the message that needs to be shared should be very specific and distinct. The Christ will need to be proclaimed.

Charles Simeon insists that the preaching of Christ is commonly used in Scripture for the publishing of the Gospel in all its parts.[208] There are some who will suggest that the Gospel of Jesus Christ is limited to what is found in 1 Corinthians 15 which refers to the death, burial, resurrection, and resurrection appearances of Christ. 1 Corinthians 15 is not intended to define the Gospel in all its parts; the rhetorical intention of 1 Corinthians 15 is to provide the argument for the bodily resurrection from the dead.[209] But for the followers of Jesus Christ, every doctrine associated with Jesus should be considered good news (the Gospel).

When the angel of the Lord came to announce the birth of Christ the Lord to the shepherds residing in the fields, the angel called it good news of great joy that will be for all the people (Luke 2:8-11). It should have been good news to those in the synagogue of Nazareth to hear from the very mouth of Jesus that He was the fulfillment of the Anointed One who Isaiah prophesied would come (Luke 4:16-20). To know that one day the same Jesus which ascended into heaven will come again in the same way, should also be good news to all who have loved His

---

[207] "G2784 – kēryssō – Concordance Results Using ESV," Blue Letter Bible, accessed April 28, 2021, https://www.blueletterbible.org/lang/lexicon/lexicon.cfm?Strongs=G2784&t=ESV.

[208] Charles Simeon, "Bible Commentaries: Charles Simeon's Horae Homileticae: Acts 8," StudyLight.org, accessed April 28, 2021, https://www.studylight.org/commentaries/eng/shh/acts-8.html#verse-5.

[209] Mark I. Wegener, "The Rhetorical Strategy of 1 Corinthians 15," *Currents in Theology and Mission* 31, no. 6 (Dec 2004): 439, accessed April 29, 2021, ATLA Religion Database with ATLASerials, EBSCOhost.

appearing (Acts 1:11, 2 Timothy 4:8). Not only should Christ's resurrection from the dead be considered good news, but every doctrine associated with the Christ should be good news to those who consider themselves to be His followers; good news that the follower of Jesus Christ should be prepared to proclaim distinctively.

It is worth reiterating from chapter one what Matthew Bates considers to be the eight stages of the gospel; how Christ preexisted with the Father [John 1:1, Philippians 2:6], how He took on human flesh [John 1:14, Philippians 2:7], how He died in accordance with the Scriptures [1 Corinthians 15:3], how He was buried, but how He was raised on the third day in accordance with the Scriptures [1 Corinthians 15:4], how He appeared to many [1 Corinthians 15:5-8], how He is currently seated at the right hand of God [Hebrews 1:3, et al.], and how He will come again as Judge [2 Timothy 4:1].[210] The followers of Jesus Christ are fulfillers of their distinctive purposes when they are willing to do more than just proclaim Christ in an abbreviated way, but willing to proclaim the gospel of Christ in all its parts.

Philip has previously been described by Luke as being full of the Holy Spirit; depicted in this writing project (according to Ephesians 5:15-18) as living life continuously and carefully according to the wisdom that is received through the understood will of the Lord. Since it is the Holy Spirit that leads and guides the followers of Jesus Christ by the wisdom of the understood will of God, then continuously and carefully living according to that wisdom is an outward expression of being full of the Holy Spirit. The distinctions associated with Philip as described in the pericope for this chapter are a manifestation of the fulness of the Spirit. Rather than going about and making known the purposes of God, Philip was being led by the Holy Spirit to a distinct location so that he might proclaim a distinct message, the Christ. For the followers of Jesus Christ who yearn to be distinctly directed by God,

---

[210.] Matthew W. Bates, Salvation by Allegiance Alone: Rethinking Faith, Works, and the Gospel of Jesus the King (Grand Rapids: Baker Academic, 2017), chap. 9, Kindle.

life must be lived continuously and carefully according to the wisdom that has been given to them by God Himself.

Franklin S. Jabini spotlights that in the first three messages that were preached by the Apostle Peter, Jesus Christ's crucifixion and resurrection was preached (c.f. Acts 2, 3, and 4).[211] The Apostle Peter took full advantage of the attention that had been gathered by the miracles and the signs that had been performed to make sure that the Lord Jesus Christ was glorified.[212] As God would have it, Philip followed suit in the city of Samaria. The chapter pericope enforces that the crowds with one accord paid attention to what was being said by Philip, when they heard him and saw the signs that he did. There is no mention of signs being performed among the others that were scattered, only by Philip who was distinctly proclaiming the Christ. As followers of Jesus Christ who desire to fulfill their distinctive purposes, we have to ponder if more miracles and signs might be performed among us if we would do more to distinctly proclaim the Christ, especially Him being crucified and being raised from the dead for the salvation of our souls.

The specific signs that were performed by Philip were the exorcism of unclean spirits and the healing of those who were paralyzed or lame. The People's Commentary emphasizes that this was a gift that was being performed by someone other than an apostle.[213] The signs that were being performed by Philip were the evidence and the enablement of the Holy Spirit that was within him. Philip was exercising the gifts that were given to him by the Holy Spirit. Just like the Apostle Peter, Philip took full advantage of the attention that had been gathered by the signs that he had been performed to ensure that the Lord Jesus was glorified

---

[211.] Franklin S. Jabini, "Preaching Christ in a Pluralistic World: The Message and Method of the Mission to Samaria in Acts 8," *Conspectus* 9 (Mar 2010): 59, accessed May 11, 2021, ATLA Religion Database with ATLASerials, EBSCOhost.

[212.] Ibid.

[213.] "Commentaries: People's Commentary (NT)," BIBLETOOLS, accessed May 13, 2021, https://www.bibletools.org/index.cfm/fuseaction/Bible.show/sVerseID/27184/eVerseID/27184/RTD/pcnt

by proclaiming Him to be the Christ. As followers of Jesus Christ, full advantage should be taken any time the exercising of our gifts seizes the attention of others to make sure that the Lord Jesus is glorified by proclaiming Him to be the Christ.

1 Peter 4:10-11 refers to the gifts that God has given to every Christ follower as a variation of God's grace and as good stewards of the variations of God's grace, our gifts should be used in order that God may be glorified through Jesus Christ in everything. Every Christ follower when provided the opportunity to exercise their God given gifts is also being provided the opportunity to proclaim Christ. John MacArthur refers to the use of our gifts for the glorification of God as the great responsibility of Christian living.[214] The great responsibility of the Christ follower is not only the exercising of their gifts, but to also ensure that God is glorified through the proclamations of Christ.

When Peter and John encountered the lame beggar at the gate of the temple (Acts 3), Peter declared that he had no silver or gold, but what he did have, he was willing to use to glorify God. What Peter had was the gift of healing that had been given to him. Peter's focus during that time and during the events that followed was not on the healing that took place, but on proclaiming Christ to those who were drawn to him when he exercised his gift.[215] Peter's intention of exalting Christ is solidified through his allusion to Isaiah 52:13 provided in Acts 3:13.[216] The intention of all Christ followers in order to fulfill their distinctive purposes should be to proclaim Christ when the exercising of their gifts seizes the attention of others so that God might be glorified.

Paul's first letter to the Corinthian church was an appeal for them to be united and to discontinue the divisions that had been established

---

[214.] John MacArthur, *The MacArthur Study Bible English Standard Version* (Wheaton, Illinois: Crossway, 2010), Introduction to 1 Peter Outline.

[215.] Jabini, 59.

[216.] Donald H. Juel, "Hearing Peter's Speech in Acts 3: Meaning and Truth in Interpretation," *Word & Word* 12, no. 1 (Wint 1992): 45, accessed May 13, 2021, ATLA Religion Database with ATLASerials, EBSCOhost.

among them because of their personal attachments to the personalities that God had sent to them. In an effort to reunite the Corinthian church, Paul redirected their affections away from the personalities that were sent to them to the message that was being preached to them, the proclamation of Jesus Christ and Him crucified (1 Corinthians 1:10 – 2:2). Donald C. Flemming maintains that the Apostle Paul did not want the Corinthian converts to maintain their attachment to the preacher, but in the power of God and His word.[217] In this same vein, the followers of Jesus Christ should make every effort to redirect any idolatrous attentions which may be directed their way by ensuring that God is glorified through the proclamations of Christ.

Luke refused to overlook the emotional response of those in the city of Samaria. God used Philip to bring much joy to the city. Though not all unclean spirits were exercised and neither were all who were paralyzed or lame healed, joy still overwhelmed the city. Galatians 5:22 categorizes joy with the fruit of the Spirit; described as being an emotion which is only relatable on the spiritual level.[218] Luke's accentuation is that what was achieved in the city was only achievable by the Holy Spirit Himself. Even though it was Philip who proclaimed Christ and it was Philip who performed the signs, Luke wanted to make certain that what was accomplished in the city could not solely be attributed to Philip. It was the Holy Spirit who was working through Philip who caused joy to overwhelm the city. In our efforts to fulfill our distinctive purposes in Christ, we should never accredit any emotional responses to what we have done; any and all emotional responses which are instigated by the exercising of our gifts should only be accredited to the Holy Spirit of God who has given us the gift.

[217.] Donald C. Flemming, "Bible Commentaries: Bridgeway Bible Commentary: 1 Corinthians 2," StudyLight.org, https://www.studylight.org/commentaries/eng/bbc/1-corinthians-2.html#copyright.

[218.] Anton ten Klooster, "Aquinas on the Fruits of the Holy Spirit as the Delight of the Christian Life," *Journal of Moral Theology* 8, (Spr 2019): 84, accessed May 14, 2021, ATLA Religion Database with ATLASerials, EBSCOhost.

In summary, God has given every Christ follower gifts that should be exercised with one intent, that God be glorified. The glorification of God should never be taken for granted but ensured through the proclamations of Christ. If Christ had not given us His Spirit, then there would be no gifts available for us to exercise. One might say that the gifts that have been given to every follower of Christ are imbedded attention getters so that the name of Christ may be proclaimed to those who are drawn by them.

CHAPTER NINE
FULFILLING GOD'S JUXTAPOSITIONAL PURPOSES

Acts 8:9-13 (ESV)

⁹ But there was a man named Simon, who had previously practiced magic in the city and amazed the people of Samaria, saying that he himself was somebody great. ¹⁰ They all paid attention to him, from the least to the greatest, saying, "This man is the power of God that is called Great." ¹¹ And they paid attention to him because for a long time he had amazed them with his magic. ¹² But when they believed Philip as he preached good news about the kingdom of God and the name of Jesus Christ, they were baptized, both men and women. ¹³ Even Simon himself believed, and after being baptized he continued with Philip. And seeing signs and great miracles performed, he was amazed.

Chapter six of this writing project is utilized to discuss the fulfillment of the contrasting purposes of God. Luke intentionally used the verses found in Acts 7:54-60 to contrast the behavior of Stephen with the hostility of those who were supposed men of faith; a contrast that resembled the radicalism of Christ.[219]

This chapter's pericope reveals God's contrasting purposes being fulfilled in the life of Philip. Only in this instance, Luke is specifically juxtaposing Philip against a magician whose name was Simon. There will be times in the life of the follower of Christ when they may find themselves juxtaposed against the ungodly for the purpose of showcasing the glory of God which is at work in them.

In Psalm 1, the psalm writer juxtaposes those who live according to the ways of the righteous with those who live according to the ways of the wicked. This juxtaposing of the righteous against the wicked is intended to describe the blessings of having an intimate relationship with the Lord by living according to the counsel of His word as opposed to living according to the destructive advisement of those that do not. Cleotha A. Robertson emphasizes the contrasting futures of the righteous versus the wicked found in Psalm 1.[220] The future of the righteous being depicted as prosperous, secure, and fruitful due to the rejection of the lifestyle and the influences of the ungodly.[221] The future of the wicked is depicted as being unstable and ending in destruction.[222]

The Prophet Ezekiel reveals the heart of the Lord God as it relates to the wicked. God's druthers are that the wicked turn from their way so that they might live rather than being destroyed (Ezekiel 18:23). God uses the juxtaposing of the righteous against the wicked so that they might be drawn to the security and stability of the righteous life. If the follower of Jesus Christ is to fulfill the juxtapositional purposes

---

[219]. Piotr Nyk, "You are Witnesses of These Things! (Luke 24:48): The Concept of Testimony in the Gospel of Luke," *Verbum Vitae* 27, (2015): 121, accessed December 23, 2020, ATLA Religion Database with ATLASerials, EBSCOhost.

[220]. Cleotha A. Robertson, "Psalm 1: A Guide for Spiritual Formation," The Living Pulpit (Online) 27, no. 1 (Spr 2018): 4, accessed May 28, 2021, ATLA Religion Database with ATLASerials, EBSCOhost.

[221]. Ibid.

[222]. Ibid., 4-5.

of God, then life has to be completely lived according to the council of God so that others might be drawn to the security and stability which is found is Christ.

Jesus Christ Himself parabolically juxtaposes a Pharisee and a tax collector who went up to the temple to pray (Luke 18:9-14). The Pharisee being a representation of those who trust in themselves for righteousness based on the works that they have done and how they compare themselves to others. The tax collector being a representation of those who acknowledge their own sinfulness before God and openly declare their need for His mercy. Jesus declares the tax collector as the one who is justified rather than the Pharisee, an inference that places the Pharisee at odds with God's estimate of him.[223] God wants to use those who maintain a humble spirit before Him to juxtapose them against those who exalt themselves as a demonstration of those who are truly justified in the sight of God.

The English Standard Version (ESV) translation of the Bible softens the ungodliness of Simon by stating that what he practiced was magic. Other translations chronicle Simon as being a practitioner of sorcery, occult arts, or witchcraft.[224] Deuteronomy 18:9-15 describes this practice as an abomination unto the Lord, an abomination that is disallowed for the people of God. The Apostle Paul refers to the practice of sorcery as the enemy of all righteousness and a perversion to the straight ways of the Lord (Acts 13:10).[225] Additionally, the practitioners of this abomination would rather listen to fortune-tellers as opposed to listening to God or to the prophets that were sent by Him; a practice that should be considered even more abominable than the practice of sorcery itself.

---

[223] Fredrick Carlson Holmgren, "The Pharisee and the Tax Collector: Luke 18:9-14 and Deuteronomy 26:1-15," *Interpretation* 48, no. 3 (Jul 1994): 253, accessed June 8, 2021, ATLA Religion Database with ATLASerials, EBSCOhost.

[224] "Acts 8:9," Bible Hub, accessed June 8, 2021, https://biblehub.com/acts/8-9.htm.

[225] Richard T. Ritenbaugh, "What the Bible Says About Diviner," BIBLETOOLS, accessed June 11, 2021, https://www.bibletools.org/index.cfm/fuseaction/Topical.show/RTD/CGG/ID/12956/Diviner.htm.

Fulfillers of the juxtapositional purposes of God always lend their ear to what the Lord has said in opposition to those who consider fortune telling a source for gaining wisdom. Those of us who have been juxtaposed against the ungodly should have a clear understanding that the primary source of our wisdom is God, the wisdom that is supplied in His word (James 1:5, Proverbs 2:6).

The author Luke provides the impetus behind Simon's occultic practices, the explicit purpose of exalting himself. Simon, in his own estimation, considered himself someone who should be highly esteemed among the Samaritan people; diagnosed by Thomas L. Brodie as someone preoccupied with greatness.[226] When the followers of Jesus Christ perceive themselves being juxtaposed against the self-exaltations of the ungodly, they should imitate the responses of Philip and make the only declarations necessary, declarations that pertain to the kingdom of God and the name of Jesus Christ (Acts 8:12).

The Apostle Paul lists sorcery as a work of the flesh which he juxtaposes against the fruits of the Spirit (Galatians 5:19-23). The Apostle Paul also identifies that the works of the flesh are accordant with those who have become conceited (Galatians 5:26). Thomas Aquinas categorizes conceit with worldly glory.[227] The Apostle Paul's assessment of those who live contrary to the Spirit appears to be consistent with Simon's self-aggrandizement in his pursuit of worldly glory. The fruit that resonates from the followers of Christ will always outshine the gratifications of the flesh especially when it is not tainted with the desire to elevate self.

Daniel 1-4 depicts the self-aggrandizements of Nebuchadnezzar, aggrandizements which included being steeped in arrogance and a

---

[226.] Thomas L. Brodie, "Towards Unraveling the Rhetorical Imitation of Sources in Acts: 2 Kgs 5 as One Component of Acts 8:9-40," Biblica 67, no. 1 (1986): 47, accessed June 11, 2021, ATLA Religion Database with ATLASerials, EBSCOhost.

[227.] Thomas Aquinas, "Patristic Bible Commentary: St. Thomas Aquinas on Galatians: Chapter 5," sites.google.com, accessed June 13, 2021, https://sites.google.com/site/aquinasstudybible/home/galatians/st-thomas-aquinas-on-galatians/chapter-1/chapter-2/chapter-3/chapter-4/chapter-5.

failure to acknowledge his accomplishments as God-given gifts in spite of prophetic warnings of judgment and pleas for repentance. Thomas Scott Cason describes the prophetic warnings of judgment and pleas for repentance as a last-ditch effort to save Nebuchadnezzar from himself.[228] God, by His grace, strategically allowed Daniel and the three Hebrew boys to become a collocation in the life of Nebuchadnezzar using them to help Nebuchadnezzar get a better glimpse of God and how He works in the lives of those who are completely surrendered to Him rather than to themselves. It was this juxtaposing that was an influence in the life of Nebuchadnezzar which ultimately caused him to extol and honor God as the King of heaven (Daniel 4:37). The juxtapositional purposes of God is to use the followers of Jesus Christ in a similar way.

Simon the sorcerer's efforts successfully managed to gain the attention of all those who lived in the city of Samaria. Max Turner professes that the people of Samaria were essentially under the domination of Simon's sorcery.[229] The attention gathered by Simon led to acclamations that exceeded what Simon was seeking for himself. The people of the city of Samaria began acknowledging Simon as the power of God. Brodie insists that this acclamation was due to Simon's own pretensions, but this observation does not align with the reading of the text.[230] The acclamation made by the people of Samaria went beyond the claims that Simon was making about himself. What can clearly be observed from the text is that Simon never rebukes the people for making such high claims about him, Simon willfully accepted it. As followers of Jesus Christ, there should never be an acceptance of adorations that exceed who we are in Christ Jesus.

[228.] Thomas Scott Carson, "Confessions of an Impotent Potentate: Reading Daniel 4 through the Lens of Ritual Punishment Theory," Journal for the Study of the Old Testament 39, no. 1 (Sep 2014): 86, accessed June 15, 2021, ATLA Religion Database with ATLASerials, EBSCOhost.

[229.] Max Turner, "Interpreting the Samaritans of Acts 8: The Waterloo of Pentecostal Soteriology and Pneumatology?" Pneuma 23, no. 2 (Fall 2001): 272, accessed June 16, 2021, ATLA Religion Database with ATLASerials, EBSCOhost.

[230.] Brodie, 4.

Acts 14:8-18 describes the elevation of adoration received by Paul and Barnabas while in the city of Lystra. The moment Paul and Barnabas heard of it, they were immediately dismayed by it and were quick to correct it, making sure the Lystrans understood that they were mere men just like them. Dean P. Bechard argues that it is the repulsed reaction of Paul and Barnabas that authenticated them as sages who had no interest in fame, only in being sharers of the gifts and wisdom that come from God.[231] When God juxtaposes the followers of Christ against those who attempt to elevate them above who they really are in Christ Jesus, then those elevations of adoration need to be quickly refuted.

The juxtaposing of Philip against Simon actually begins in the pericopal focus of chapter eight of this writing project. In Acts 8:4-8, Luke provides that it was the distinctive proclamations of Christ and the signs that Philip performed that gained the attention of all those in the city of Samaria. The pericope for this chapter describes that previous to Philip's arrival, it was Simon who held the attention of the Samaritans through his own self-aggrandizements and the sorcery that he performed. The pericope for this chapter also informs us that the proclamations of Philip and the signs that he performed evolved into more than just being an attention grabber. The proclamations of Philip and the signs that he performed precipitated into a belief by them all in the good news about the kingdom of God and the name of Jesus Christ. The kingdom of God principally being God's personal presence in power and rule over those who receive it and the name of Jesus Christ being the only name by which men can be saved (Acts 4:12).[232] The desire and the goal for the followers of Jesus Christ should be to do more than simply capture the attention of others with their proclamations and God-given gifts; the desire and the goal should be that the attention

---

[231.] Dean Philip Bechard, "Paul Among the Rustics: The Lystran Episode (Acts 14:8-20) and Lucan Apologetic," *The Catholic Biblical Quarterly* 63, no. 1 (Jan 2001): 96, accessed June 16, 2021, ATLA Religion Database with ATLASerials, EBSCOhost.

[232.] Turner, 276.

that we capture will lead to a belief in the kingdom of God and the name of Jesus Christ.

God's will for His children is to shine as lights in this crooked and perverse generation as they hold fast to the word of life (Philippians 2:15-16), shining in such a way that men may see their good deeds and glorify the Father which is in heaven (Matthew 5:16). Margaret Mowczko expresses that holding fast to the word of life illuminates the path to Christ hopefully leading people to Christ.[233] Fulfilling God's juxtapositional purposes provides the opportunity for those who are lost to come to a saving faith in Jesus Christ and a desire to surrender their lives to the will of God.

The only sin expressly identified in the chapter pericope is the sin of Simon, but the Scriptures clearly state that all have sinned and fall short of the glory of God (Romans 3:23). Falling short of the glory of God is expounded upon by Dane C. Ortlund as a deficiency in the image of which God intended when He created us.[234] Therefore, all who believed needed to hear the good news of the saving grace of Jesus Christ, the One who was sent to save us from our sins (Matthew 1:21). Philip's expanded purpose exceeded being juxtaposed against Simon, Philip was sent to the city of Samaria to be a blessing to them all. Simon was drawing others to himself, but Philip was being used of God to draw others to Himself (John 6:44). John 6:44 contextually summarized as the draw of God to salvation.[235] As followers of Jesus Christ, wherever God sends us or allows us to go, our expanded purpose is to be a blessing to all through the use of our God-given gifts and our

---

[233.] Marg Mowczko, "Living as Lights in the World – Philippians 2:12-18," Marg Mowczko: Exploring the Biblical Theology of Christian Egalitarianism, accessed June 18, 2021, https://margmowczko.com/philippians-2_12-18/.

[234.] Dane C. Ortlund, "What Does it Mean to Fall Short of the Glory of God? Romans 3:23 in Biblical-Theological Perspective," *The Westminster Theological Journal* 80, accessed June 18, 2021, ATLA Religion Database with ATLASerials, EBSCOhost.

[235.] "What Does It Mean that God Draws Us to Salvation?" Got Questions: Your Questions: Biblical Answers, Got Questions Ministries, last updated April 26, 2021, https://www.gotquestions.org/drawn-salvation.html.

proclamations of Jesus the Christ with the hope that someone will be drawn to salvation.

Luke informs us that the belief of the Samaritans led to the baptism of them all. Chapter six of this writing project discusses the three distinctions of baptism, the baptism of water, the baptism of the Holy Spirit and fire, and the baptism of all that Christ has commanded. It was Philips preaching that baptized the Samaritans in all that Christ had commanded (or more explicitly the truths of Scripture) and the Samaritans baptism of the Holy Spirit was yet a future event (to be discussed in the next chapter). Therefore, this baptism was the baptism of water, the public demonstration of one's allegiance to Christ; also defined as a ceremonial dipping.[236] A ceremonial dipping that should be considered necessary to the follower of Jesus Christ due to its association by Jesus Christ with the fulfillment of all righteousness (Matthew 3:15).

It is worth noting that there is no mention of who performed the baptisms. The Samaritans were baptized based on their belief in the kingdom of God and in the name of Jesus Christ. The who of those that perform baptisms is insignificant in comparison to the Who that we are being baptized in the name of, the name of Jesus Christ.[237]

The chapter pericope closes emphasizing Simon the sorcerer's apparent belief and baptism. Luke rhetorically emphasizes that all of the other Samaritans that were baptized believed in the good news about the kingdom of God and the name of Jesus Christ. As it relates to Simon, his continuing focus was not on the good news that was being preached, but on the signs and the great miracles that Philip was performing. Simon's focus was not on the One in whom his faith

---

[236] "907. baptizō: Strong's Concordance," Bible Hub, accessed June 22, 2021, https://biblehub.com/greek/907.htm.

[237] Michael Strickland, "The (In)Significance of The Baptizer in the Early Church: The Importance of Baptism and Unimportance of the One who Baptized," Journal of the Evangelical Theological Society 61, no. 2 (Jun 2018): 355-366, accessed June 23, 2021, ATLA Religion Database with ATLASerials, EBSCOhost.

was supposed to be placed, Simon's focus was on the works that were being done. As followers of Jesus Christ, it behooves us to have an understanding of what the focus is of those who continue with us. Is their focus and their faith on Jesus Christ or is it on the works that are being done? God does not juxtapose the followers of Christ so that their works will be glorified. God juxtaposes the follower of Christ so that the name of Jesus will be glorified.

In sum, God's will for the followers of Christ is to juxtapose them against the ungodly for the purpose of showcasing the glory of God which is at work in them. A glory which is revealed through living a life of humility before God; a life that is dependent on the wisdom that is found in God's word and not upon the wisdom that is in the world (1 Corinthians 3:19). God uses His juxtapositional purposes to draw the ungodly to the security and stability that is found in living a righteous life, the life that is found in Christ.

CHAPTER TEN
Fulfilling God's Deferential Purposes

Acts 8:14-25 (ESV)

[14] *Now when the apostles at Jerusalem heard that Samaria had received the word of God, they sent to them Peter and John, [15] who came down and prayed for them that they might receive the Holy Spirit, [16] for he had not yet fallen on any of them, but they had only been baptized in the name of the Lord Jesus. [17] Then they laid their hands on them and they received the Holy Spirit. [18] Now when Simon saw that the Spirit was given through the laying on of the apostles› hands, he offered them money, [19] saying, "Give me this power also, so that anyone on whom I lay my hands may receive the Holy Spirit." [20] But Peter said to him, "May your silver perish with you, because you thought you could obtain the gift of God with money! [21] You have neither part nor lot in this matter, for your heart is not right before God. [22] Repent, therefore, of this wickedness of yours, and pray to the Lord that, if possible, the intent of your heart may be forgiven you. [23] For I see that you are in the gall of bitterness and in the bond of iniquity." [24] And Simon answered, "Pray for me to the Lord, that nothing of what you have said may come upon me."*

25 Now when they had testified and spoken the word of the Lord, they returned to Jerusalem, preaching the gospel to many villages of the Samaritans.

What may not be immediately obvious in this chapter's pericope is how Philip takes a step back. Philip becomes an active observer rather than an active participant. Though God used Philip in a mighty way in the city of Samaria to preach Christ and to exercise the gifts that he had been given, when the apostles Peter and John made their appearance, Philip quietly and unassumingly deferred to them.

Kyle A. Keefer labels the efforts of Philip as wildly successful.[238] Even though the efforts of Philip through the power of the Holy Spirit resulted in a fair amount of success, Philip was moved to take a step back. No matter how extensively God may use the followers of Christ, there will be times when the right response is to defer to others.

1 Timothy 5:17 prescribes that the elders who rule well are worthy of double honor, especially those who labor in preaching and teaching; one of the contextual implications of double honor being a high level of respect.[239] Peter and John were numbered with the apostles who provided the doctrines that edified the early church and offered the guidance that resulted in Philip being numbered with the seven. One might say that as a demonstration of honor and respect, Philip deferred to Peter and John. In the same manner, the follower of Christ should not consider it shameful to defer to those who were and are being used to mature them in Christ, especially when deferment may be providing the opportunity for those being deferred to being used of God as well.

The Apostle Paul described the work that is done by the servants of God as a work that is often done in tandem (1 Corinthians 3:5-7). The

---

[238]. Kyle A. Keefer, "Philip, Samaria, and God's Plan," America: The Jesuit Review, accessed June 28, 2021, https://www.americamagazine.org/content/good-word/philip-samaria-and-gods-plan.

[239]. "What Does 1 Timothy 5:17 Mean?" BibleRef.com, accessed July 1, 2021, https://www.bibleref.com/1-Timothy/5/1-Timothy-5-17.html#commentary.

Apostle Paul describes both himself and Apollos as servants who were used of God to lead the Corinthians to a belief in Christ; instruments of God being used to bring the Corinthians to faith.[240] Paul elucidates that God used him to plant and He used Apollos to water, but in humiliation and glorification Paul also provides that without God there would be no growth; growth that would be a continual act of God throughout the lives of the Corinthians.[241] The tandem acts of planting and watering were acts that were performed as the Lord had assigned (1 Corinthians 3:5). Philip deferred to Peter and John so that the work that had been assigned to them might be accomplished to the glory of God.

The level of the effectiveness of Philip's work in the city of Samaria, or even better stated, the work that the Holy Spirit was doing through Philip is indicated by the news of it being heard in Jerusalem. Luke provides no indication of Philip doing anything intentional to assure that what had been done was heard of in Jerusalem. Luke simply states that the news of what had been done made its way to Jerusalem. When the Holy Spirit is at work in the lives of the people of God, no self-advertisement is necessary. The work of the Holy Spirit that is being done through the people of God will advertise itself.

Luke reports in Luke 4:14 that the fame of Jesus spread throughout the surrounding regions of Galilee (KJV). Luke precedes this observation by emphasizing that Jesus' return to Galilee was in the power of the Spirit; an emphasis that is intended to characterize the ministry of Jesus in completeness.[242] The same power that was at work in Jesus Christ is the same power that is at work in every individual that is truly a child of God, especially when they are doing the work that the Lord has assigned. When that same power is at work, then the work will

---

[240] "Spiritual Maturity," Grace Covenant Church, accessed July 2, 2021, https://gracegi.org/sermons/spiritual-maturity-1-corinthians-31-9/.

[241] "Spiritual Maturity."

[242] Gary H. Everett, "Bible Commentaries: Gary H. Everett Study Notes on the Holy Scriptures: Luke 4," StudyLight.org, accessed July 2, 2021, https://www.studylight.org/commentaries/eng/ghe/luke-4.html#verse-14.

advertise itself; no billboards, no commercials, or any form of self-advertisement will be necessary.

There is an Old Testament principal that provides the mandate for responding to incidences that have only been rumored and not personally experienced. Both Deuteronomy 13:12-18 and 17:2-7 insist upon diligent inquiry being made prior to taking the necessary actions that have been commanded by God; necessary actions that can only be taken after the truth has been determined by two or three witnesses. Joshua Berman labels this required response as the Deuteronomic call for due process.[243] This may be the very thing that motivated the apostles to send Peter and John to the city of Samaria.

As wonderful and as exciting as it must have been to hear about the Samaritans reception of the word of God, for the apostles this was mere rumor. Philip's deferment provided Peter and John ample time to determine if what they had heard was based on truth. As followers of Jesus Christ, we do not take action simply based on what we have heard. God requires us to do our due diligence to substantiate that what we have heard is indeed true. Proverbs 14:15 states that the simple believe everything, but the prudent gives thought to his steps; God inspired words that save us from gullibility.[244] The thoughts that our steps should be based on are thoughts that align with truth.

The deduction that may be concluded about the actions of Peter and John after their arrival in Samaria is that they both believe that what they had heard was found to be true. They both prayed that the Samaritans might receive the Holy Ghost. The prayer that the Samaritans might receive the Holy Spirit affirms Peter and John's belief that the Samaritans had truly received the word of God that had been preached to them.

---

[243] Joshua Berman, "CTH 133 and the Hittite Provenance of Deuteronomy 13," *Journal of Biblical Literature* 130, no. 1 (Spr 2011): 38, accessed July 4, 2021, ATLA Religion Database with ATLASerials, EBSCOhost.

[244] "Proverbs 14:15," LetGodbeTrue.com, accessed July 5, 2021, https://letgodbetrue.com/proverbs/index/chapter-14/proverbs-14-15/.

In his exposition of 1 Thessalonians 2:13, John Piper surmises that there is a right way to receive the word of God.[245] The right way to receive the word of God is not by accepting it as the word of men, but by accepting it for what it really is, the word of God.[246] Peter and John's investigation revealed that Philip's proclamations about the Christ had not been accepted as merely the word that came from Philip, but as the very word that came from God.

David Guzik connects the sending of Peter and John to Jesus giving Peter the keys of the kingdom of heaven (Matthew 16:19), but the more explicit connection is Jesus' response to Peter's confession (Matthew 16:16-18).[247] Jesus' response was that Peter's confession was not based on a revelation that he received from flesh and blood, but it was a revelation that he received from the Father who is in heaven. It would be by this same revelation upon which Jesus would build His church. The Samaritans did not receive Philip's proclamations of Christ as though they were revelations provided by flesh and blood; the Samaritans received Philip's proclamations as the very word that came from God.

After being convinced that the Samaritans did indeed receive the word of God as the word of God, Peter and John prayed that the Samaritans might receive the Holy Spirit. The extent of Peter and John's power was the ability to pray that the Samaritans might receive the Holy Spirit. Epitomized by Yuri Phanon as the enablement to participate in God's mission; the endowment of power for life and service.[248] For the

---

[245]. John Piper, "How to Receive the Word of Man as the Word of God," desiringGod, accessed July 6, 2021, https://www.desiringgod.org/messages/how-to-receive-the-word-of-man-as-the-word-of-god.

[246]. Ibid.

[247]. David Guzik, "Study Guide for Acts 8," Blue Letter Bible, accessed July 6, 2021, https://www.blueletterbible.org/Comm/guzik_david/StudyGuide2017-Act/Act-8.cfm?a=1026014.

[248]. Yuri Phanon, "The Work of the Holy Spirit in the Conception, Baptism and Temptation of Christ: Implications for the Pentecostal Christian 1," *Asian Journal of Pentecostal Studies* 20, no. 1 (Feb 2017): 37, accessed July 9, 2021, ATLA Religion Database with ATLASerials, EBSCOhost.

Samaritans to actually receive the Holy Spirit, that would have to be an act of the exalted Jesus Christ Himself.

Through John the Baptist's testimony, we learn the limitations of his power, to baptize with water for repentance. But we also learn, that it would be the One on whom the Spirit would descend and remain who would baptize with the Holy Spirit, Jesus the Lamb of God who takes away the sins of the world (John 1:19-34).

Phanon connects the remaining of the Spirit upon Jesus as His enablement to baptize others with the Holy Spirit, but it is hard to overlook John the Baptist's revelation of Jesus as the Lamb of God that takes away the sins of the world as an important connection to this enablement as well.[249] If Jesus had not been willing to die for our sins, then He ultimately would not have been exalted. If Jesus had not been exalted, then He would not have received the enablement to pour out the promise of the Holy Spirit (Acts 2:33). It is Jesus the Lamb of God who takes away the sins of the world who received the enablement to pour out the promise of the Holy Spirit. When Peter and John prayed, they were asking Christ to do what only He had the power to do.

In Peter's message on the day of Pentecost after being filled with the Holy Spirit himself, Peter admonished those who heard him to repent, that each one should be baptized in the name of Jesus for the forgiveness of their sins, and they would receive the gift of the Holy Ghost (Acts 2:38). Paul Elbert tags Peter's speech as programmatic, Spirit- reception language.[250] Elbert also reminds us that Peter's programmatic speech is immediately quantified by identifying it with "the promise" (Acts 2:39); the promise that the sending of the Holy Spirit would be accomplished by Jesus Christ Himself (Luke 24:49).[251]

---

[249] Ibid., 53.

[250] Paul Elbert, "Acts 2:38 in Light of the Syntax of Imperative—Future Passive and Imperative—Present Participle Combinations," *The Catholic Biblical Quarterly* 75, no. 1 (Jan 2013): 95, accessed July 13, 2021, ATLA Religion Database with ATLASerials, EBSCOhost.

[251] Ibid.

The repentance of the Samaritans is evidenced through their turning away from Simon and his works of sorcery and receiving the gospel of the kingdom God and the name of Jesus Christ. The Samaritans had also been baptized in the name of the Lord Jesus. Peter and John were now praying and laying hands on the Samaritans in pursuit of God's confirmation that the Samaritans had sincerely accepted the call of God to Himself (Acts 2:39). The confirmation is revealed through the Samaritans receiving the Holy Spirit.

The wording of the text may infer that Simon was excluded from receiving the Holy Spirit. There are no textual indications of his repentance. The previous chapter's pericope identified Simon as someone who used sorcery to justify his self-proclamations of being someone great. This same Simon accepted the acclamations of being someone great, even the acclamation of being the power of God. After Simon's baptism, his draw was not to the word of God but to the signs and miracles being performed by Philip.

Similarly in this chapter's pericope, Simon continues his pursuit for personal greatness through his desire to obtain the power that only belongs to God. Rather than surrendering to the power of God, Simon wanted to obtain power so that he might continue as he was. Some commentators believe that Simon's offer of money was his attempt to buy himself an apostleship.[252] Simon was perverting the grace of God and denying the Master and Lord, Jesus Christ (Jude 4).[253] Simon was still Simon; no evidence of repentance.

Luther B. McIntyre argues that repentance is the necessary action for the forgiveness of sins.[254] Coinciding with this argument, repentance would also be the necessary action for receiving the Holy Spirit.

[252.] "Forerunner Commentary," BIBLETOOLS, accessed July 15, 2021, https://www.bibletools.org/index.cfm/fuseaction/Bible.show/sVerseID/27190/eVerseID/27190.

[253.] Ibid.

[254.] Luther B. McIntyre Jr, "Baptism and Forgiveness in Acts 2:38," Bibliotheca sacra 153, no. 609 (Jan-Mar 1996): 57, accessed July 14, 2021, ATLA Religion Database with ATLASerials, EBSCOhost.

Textual evidence provides no indication of Simon's repentance. Without the necessary action of repentance, the most likely outcome was that Simon was excluded from receiving the Holy Spirit.

The argument for Simon's failure to repent is strengthened in Peter's response to Simon. Peter openly states that Simon's behavior was birthed from his own thoughts. Peter says that Simon thought that he could obtain the gift of God with money. Even though Simon observed that the receiving of the Holy Spirit was not connected to a financial transaction, he still thought that he could pay for it. Simon remained captive to his own thoughts rather than surrendering to how God made Himself known (2 Corinthians 10:5). Simon exalted his own thinking over true knowledge and understanding.[255]

Secondly, Peter tells Simon that he neither has part nor lot in this matter. Jabini informs us that the Greek word translated as "matter" is logos.[256] Peter is distinctively saying that unlike the other Samaritans, Simon had not received the word of God as the word of God.

Thirdly, Peter tells Simon that his heart was not right before God and that he needed to repent so that the intent of his heart might be forgiven. Peter was stressing the issue of Simon's unchanged heart. Repentance is a change of heart that leads to a change in the direction of life (Joel 2:12-13).[257] The direction of Simon's life had not changed.

Lastly, Peter says that Simon was in the gall of bitterness and in the bond of iniquity. David Brown categorizes the gall of bitterness and the bond of iniquity as expressions that describe the awfulness of Simon's

---

[255] John W. Ritenbaugh, "Commentaries: Forerunner Commentary: 2 Corinthians 10:3-5," BIBLETOOLS, accessed July 15, 2021, https://www.bibletools.org/index.cfm/fuseaction/Bible.show/sVerseID/28977/eVerseID/28977/version/gnb.

[256] Jabini, 57.

[257] Paul Coxall, "Repentance: A Change of Heart, a Change in Direction," UtG: Understanding the Gospel (blog), July 22, 2020, accessed July 20, 2021, https://understandingthegospel.org/blogs/paul-coxall/repentance-a-change-of-heart-a-change-in-direction/.

condition and his captivity to it.[258] Toussaint believes that the gall of bitterness is an echo of Deuteronomy 29:18 which contextually refers to someone who is walking in the stubbornness of their own heart.[259] Each one of these statements is descriptive of Simon's failure to repent excluding him from receiving the Holy Spirit.

Simon's answer to Peter may also be an indication of the bleakness of Simon's condition. Peter admonished Simon to pray to the Lord so that the intent of his heart might be forgiven, but Simon solicited Peter to pray to the Lord for him so that he might not suffer the consequences for his actions. Simon appears to be unconcerned about receiving the Lord's forgiveness; Simon's response reveals only a desire not to suffer the consequences for his actions.

Repentance and prayer are both connected to the forgiveness of sin and the desire to turn away from it. Peter's programmatic speech, as discussed earlier in this chapter, insists upon repentance and baptism for the forgiveness of sin. 1 John 1:9 provides that if we confess our sins, God is faithful and just to forgive us of our sin and He is willing to cleanse us from all unrighteousness. Interestingly enough, 1 John 1:10 provides that an unwillingness to acknowledge sin which contextually is connected to an unwillingness to confess sin is an indication that God's word is not in us. Simon's desire to only be absolved of sin's consequences rather than receiving the forgiveness of sin is an intimation that Simon did not receive the word of God as the word of God.

The chapter pericope ends by sharing the enhancement to the apostle's ministry. Previous to this occasion, the Holy Spirit-filled apostles had not ministered the word of God to anyone outside of Jerusalem (Acts 8:1). This occasion provided the opportunity for the apostles to testify and speak the word of the Lord in the city of Samaria and to

---

[258] David Brown, "The Acts of the Apostles: Commentary by David Brown: Chapter 8," Blue Letter Bible, accessed July 16, 2021, https://www.blueletterbible.org/Comm/jfb/Act/Act_008.cfm?a=1026023.

[259] Toussaint, 374.

preach the gospel to many of the villages of Samaria as they made their return to Jerusalem.

An interesting association that seems appropriate at this conjecture is that Peter and John did not preach the gospel in any of the villages of Samaria on their way to the city of Samaria, but it would appear that this occasion fueled Peter and John to preach the gospel to the villages of Samaria on their return journey. One might even go as far as to say that Philip's deferment to Peter and John played a role in the enhancement to Peter and John's ministry. One of the benefits in fulfilling the deferential purposes of God is that it may play an integral part in the enhancement of someone else's ministry.

What this immediately calls to mind is John the Baptist's famous statement of deferment as it related to Jesus Christ. John said that He must increase, but I must decrease. For John, his deferral resulted in his joy being fulfilled (John 3:29-30). This deferential response is in sharp contrast to those who were considered the Jerusalem elite who instead of joy responded with envy.[260] The follower of Jesus Christ, should find joy in deferring to others when the occasion deems it to be the appropriate response because it may result in the enhancement of someone else's ministry.

The purpose of deferment is not only fulfilled in subordinate roles, but it can also be applicable in superordinate roles as well. Some of the greatest ministerial advice given to Moses was the advisement to defer to others. Rather than being the single source available to judge matters and disputes that arose among God's people, Moses' father-in-law Jethro advised him to assign able, God-fearing men to be judges over small matters while he himself would judge the hard cases (Exodus

---

[260.] Jerome H. Neyrey, S.J. and Richard L Rohrbaugh, "He Must Increase, I Must Decrease (John 3:30): A Cultural and Social Interpretation" *The Catholic Biblical Quarterly* 63, no. 3 (Jul 2001): 465, accessed July 16, 2021, ATLA Religion Database with ATLASerials, EBSCOhost.

18:13-26). Theologians refer to this as the Jethro Principle.[261] Moses' deferment to those who would be considered his subordinates relieved him of a necessary, but heavy burden that he was trying to accomplish on his own. Fulfilling the deferential purposes of God, can be a blessing to those in superordinate roles by relieving them of the stress that is associated with accomplishing difficult tasks alone.

In summary, taking a step back or deferring to others may be the more accurate response as circumstances dictate. Fulfilling the deferential purposes of God can be a demonstration of honor and respect. Deference may be providing the opportunity for others to be used of God so that their ministry might be enhanced. Deference also provides the blessing of stress relief to those who have been trying to accomplish difficult tasks on their own.

[261.] Leesa Renée, "The Jethro Principle: The 3 Things You Can Do to Become a Better Leader in Your Ministry or Business," LEESA RENÉE: Exploring Bias One Question at a Time, accessed July 19, 2021, ATLA Religion Database with ATLASerials, EBSCOhost.

CHAPTER ELEVEN
Fulfilling God's Transitional Purposes

Acts 8:26-31 (ESV)

²⁶ Now an angel of the Lord said to Philip, "Rise and go toward the south to the road that goes down from Jerusalem to Gaza." This is a desert place. ²⁷ And he rose and went. And there was an Ethiopian, a eunuch, a court official of Candace, queen of the Ethiopians, who was in charge of all her treasure. He had come to Jerusalem to worship ²⁸ and was returning, seated in his chariot, and he was reading the prophet Isaiah. ²⁹ And the Spirit said to Philip, "Go over and join this chariot." ³⁰ So Philip ran to him and heard him reading Isaiah the prophet and asked, "Do you understand what you are reading?" ³¹ And he said, "How can I, unless someone guides me?" And he invited Philip to come up and sit with him.

The chapter pericope begins by notifying us that Philip's ministry in the city of Samaria had reached its conclusion and there are no Scriptural indications that Philip would ever return. Chuck Smith acknowledges how the Holy Spirit used Philip to ignite a great revival in the city of Samaria.[262] Guzik also acknowledges the great success of Philip's ministry in Samaria.[263] But as God would have it, it was time for Philip to transition out of this successful ministry to a desert place on a road that led to Gaza. The observation that seems quite plain is that there is the possibility that God will transition us out of a successful ministerial position and direct us to places where success from human perspectives seems doubtful.

Jennie Bain Wilson authored the words to the gospel hymn, "Hold to God's Unchanging Hand."[264] The first stanza of the hymn shares these words:

> Time is filled with swift transition.
>
> Naught of earth unmoved can stand.
>
> Build your hopes on things eternal.
>
> Hold to God's unchanging hand.[265]

The association is it relates to ministry is that there are those who find themselves in positions of ministry that are stable and long term, but for the majority of the followers of Jesus Christ, ministerial opportunities will be filled with swift transitions. As we hold to God's unchanging hand, He leads and guides us to the work that He has preordained for

---

[262] Chuck Smith, "Chuck Smith: Study Guide for Acts," Blue Letter Bible, accessed July 23, 2021, https://www.blueletterbible.org/Comm/smith_chuck/StudyGuides_Acts/Acts.cfm?a=1026026.

[263] David Guzik, "Study Guide for Acts 8," Blue Letter Bible, accessed July 23, 2021, https://www.blueletterbible.org/Comm/guzik_david/StudyGuide2017-Act/Act-8.cfm?a=1026026.

[264] Jennie Bain Wilson, "Hold to God's Unchanging Hand," Hymnary.org, accessed July 23, 2021, https://hymnary.org/text/time_is_filled_with_swift_transition.

[265] Ibid.

us to do (Ephesians 2:10). We should be ready and prepared to fulfill God's transitional purposes especially as it relates to ministry.

What might be considered the model for this perspective in ministry is found in Acts 8:1, 4. The apostles, for the most part, remained in Jerusalem, but those who were scattered went throughout the regions of Judea and Samaria preaching the word. Most churches, whether knowingly or unknowingly, follow this model. Once congregations are dismissed, congregants scatter to their various destinations and what they should be doing is readying and preparing themselves to fulfill God's transitional purposes in ministry wherever they might find themselves, leaving behind the few that provide ministerial services within the walls of the church.

Luke details that it was an angel of the Lord who commanded Philip to go toward the south to the road that goes down from Jerusalem to Gaza. Zorodzai Dube identifies the angel of the Lord as the Holy Spirit Himself.[266] Jim Loepp Thiessen identifies the angel of the Lord in the same way.[267] This theology aligns with those who believe that the angel of the Lord is a phrase that is formed as an appositional construct (also called a definitional construct); the second word being used to identify the first.[268] The best resultant translation for those who believe that the angel of the Lord is an appositional construct would be "the angel that is the Lord."[269]

Whether this argument holds water or not in this case, the intent is that the message or the commandment that Philip received came

---

[266] Zorodzai Dube, "The Ethiopian Eunuch in Transit: A Migrant Theoretical Perspective," Hervormde Teologiese Studies 69, no. 1 (2013): 2, accessed July 25, 2021, ATLA Religion Database with ATLASerials, EBSCOhost.

[267] Jim Loepp Thiessen, " What's Stopping You? Philip and the Ethiopian Eunuch (Acts 8:25-39)," Vision (Winnipeg, Man) 4, no. 2 (Fall 2003): 54, accessed July 25, 2021, ATLA Religion Database with ATLASerials, EBSCOhost.

[268] Andrew S. Malone, "Distinguishing the Angel of the Lord," *Bulletin for Biblical Research* 21, no. 3 (2011): 301, accessed July 25, 2021, ATLA Religion Database with ATLASerials, EBSCOhost.

[269] Ibid.

from the Lord Himself. As followers of the Lord Jesus Christ, when we receive a commandment from the Lord, whether it comes to us directly or in an indirect way, the response should still be the same; we should obey it. Maybe this was Luke's intent in supplying such an indefinite identification for the angel of the Lord at this point; not to emphasize the identity of the angel of the Lord but to highlight Philip's response; he rose and went.

The location where Philip was commanded to go is described as a desert place. From the human perspective, an unlikely place for successful ministry. The potential of a successful ministry should never be assessed by human perspectives. Success is the precipitant of obedience to what God has commanded while trusting in His leadership and guidance (Proverbs 3:1-6); trust being the demanded condition for success.[270] Philip's successful ministry did not cease because God transitioned him out of the city of Samaria, it actually persisted because he obeyed what God had commanded. Fulfilling God's transitional purposes results in the continuance of successful ministry.

Obedience to what God had commanded led Philip to his next God-given ministerial assignment, an Ethiopian eunuch. Philip, being of Jewish decent, found himself being used of God to minister to those who were outside of his ethnicity and his culture; the Samaritans of mixed Jewish descent and this Ethiopian eunuch of African descent.[271] As fulfillers of God's transitional purposes, we may find ourselves doing the same; ministering to those who are outside of our ethnicity and outside of our own cultural influences.

By the admission of the Apostle Peter, the Jews believed that it was unlawful for them to associate or visit anyone of another nation (Acts 10:28); a law which is believed to be more of a traditional Pharisaism

---

[270.] Norman C. Habel, "Symbolism of Wisdom in Proverbs 1-9," *Interpretation* 26, no. 2 (Apr 1972): 146, accessed July 25, 2021, ATLA Religion Database with ATLASerials, EBSCOhost.

[271.] Herbert Lockyer, Sr., ed., *Nelson's Illustrated Bible Dictionary* (Nashville: Thomas Nelson Publishers, 1986), 942.

rather than from the law itself.²⁷² Through a vision, God revealed to Peter that no one should be called common whom God has made clean (Acts 10:15). Strong's Concordance furnishes that the usage of the word common in this context means to be regarded or treated as unclean.²⁷³ Clarity of understanding was provided to Peter through his interactions with Cornelius the Roman centurion (Acts 10:1) along with Cornelius' relatives, and his close friends who had gathered themselves together to hear what Peter had been commanded by God to say to them (Acts 10: 24, 33). While Peter preached to them about Christ, the Holy Spirit fell upon all those who had gathered to hear his message (Acts 10:44). Abraham Friesen suggests that it was through the pouring out of the Holy Spirit upon this gathering that Peter now clearly understood that just as those of Jewish descent had been cleansed by the Holy Spirit, God is also willing to do to those who are of a different ethnicity and culture.²⁷⁴ Fulfillment of God's transitional purposes means being ready and willing to share Christ with those who are of a different ethnicity and culture.

Psalm 67 shares that God's graciousness and His blessings are shined upon the people of God so that they may make known His ways upon the earth and His saving power among all nations. Nissim Amzallag observes that the substantial part of Psalm 67 is its reference to all nations.²⁷⁵ God's transitional purposes will not be fulfilled if there is no willingness to be a witness to those whose ethnicity and culture are unlike their own.

[272.] "Ellicott's Commentary for English Readers," Bible Hub, accessed August 8, 2021, https://biblehub.com/commentaries/ellicott/acts/10.htm.

[273.] "2840. koinoó: Strong's Concordance," Bible Hub, accessed July 30, 2021, https://biblehub.com/greek/2840.htm.

[274.] Abraham Friesen, "Acts 10: The Baptism of Cornelius as Interpreted by Thomas Müntzer and Felix Manz," *The Mennonite Quarterly Review* 64, no. 1 (Jan 1990): 7, accessed July 30, 2021, ATLA Religion Database with ATLASerials, EBSCOhost.

[275.] Gérard Nissim Amzallag, "Psalm 67 and the Cosmopolite Musical Worship of YHWH," *Bulletin for Biblical Research* 25, no. 2 (2015): 172, accessed July 30, 2021, ATLA Religion Database with ATLASerials, EBSCOhost.

Philip's next God-given assignment transitioned him from ministering to a large number of individuals to ministering to just one. This Ethiopian eunuch was so important to God that He led Philip solely to him. For those of us who are citizens of the kingdom of God, there may be times and opportunities when God may lead us away from the masses to minister to just one.

The parable found in Luke 15, which is often mistaken for three parables (Luke 15:3), emphasizes the explosion of joy when just one sinner repents. Gerald L. Stevens considers the explosion of joy as a preview of the eschatological joy that is to come in the kingdom of God; a joy that God allows us to experience the moment one sinner repents.[276]

Not only did Jesus' ministry reach out to the masses, but He also took the time to minister to just one (e.g., John 4). Since a servant is not greater than His master (John 13:16), then as the servants of Christ we should eagerly accept the opportunities to minister to just one especially knowing the potential of the joy that may be ignited on earth and in heaven.

Luke identifies the Ethiopian eunuch as a court official who was in charge of the queen's treasury. In later verses, Luke describes the Ethiopian eunuch as an official who had others in his command (Acts 8:38); a command which appears to have extended beyond the execution of official business. The chapter pericope details that the Ethiopian eunuch had come from Jerusalem, not on official business, but to worship. Dube describes the Ethiopian eunuch as someone who held a position that endowed him with many privileges; privileges that were both personal and official.[277]

Even the chariot by which the eunuch travelled was a reflection of his higher social position.[278] Philip traveled by foot, but the eunuch

---

[276] Gerald L. Stevens, "Luke 15: Parables of God's Search for Sinners," The Theological Educator 56, (Fall 1997): 75, accessed July 30, 2021, ATLA Religion Database with ATLASerials, EBSCOhost.

[277] Dube, 4.

[278] Dube, 3.

travelled by chariot. Fulfillment of our transitional purposes may find us ministering to those who have a higher status in this life than we do ourselves.

Proverbs 18:16 (NKJV) dictates that a man's gift makes room for him and brings him before great men. The Pulpit Commentary notes that the word "gift" in this verse has been taken in different senses, but if there is any contextuality in the book of Proverbs, then the gift spoken of in Proverbs 18:16 is described in the verse that precedes it.[279] The gift is the knowledge that the prudent and the wise both seek after and acquire (Proverbs 18:15). God may at times want to use the Biblical knowledge that has been sought after and acquired by His children to minister to those who have achieved a higher life status than their own. The Apostles Peter and John were perceived as being uneducated, common men, but God used the knowledge that they had acquired to minister to the high priest, rulers, elders, and scribes; those who were considered scholars in their day (Acts 4:5-12). Just like Peter and John, God wants to use the followers of Jesus Christ to minister to those who may be of a higher life status than their own and so it was with Philip.

The continuance of the pericope establishes the identity of the one who was previously referenced as an angel of the Lord. It was the Spirit Himself that was speaking to Philip. The argument for the angel of the Lord being the Spirit Himself is strengthened by the unmediated commands that were given to Philip.[280]

Philip's ministerial assignment became evident once he came near to the chariot. Philip heard the Ethiopian eunuch reading Isaiah the prophet. It was this reading that prompted Philip to ask do you understand what you are reading. It was Philip who opened the door for the opportunity to provide ministry to this Ethiopian eunuch. There will

---

[279] "Pulpit Commentary," Bible Hub, accessed August 3, 2021, https://biblehub.com/commentaries/pulpit/proverbs/18.htm.

[280] Stephen L. White, "Angel of the Lord: Messenger or Euphemism?" Tyndale Bulletin 50, no. 2 (1999): 302, accessed August 4, 2021, ATLA Religion Database with ATLASerials, EBSCOhost.

be times in the life of a Christ follower when God will use them to open the door for ministerial opportunities.

Jesus did not wait for the woman at the well to initiate conversations with Him, Jesus initiated the conversations which opened the door to minister to her (John 4:7). As Christ followers, we should put aside timidity and be willing to initiate conversation in the hopes that it will provide an open door for ministry.

The Ethiopian eunuch's response is what actually provided the clarification of why Philip was commanded to this desert place at this particular time. The Ethiopian eunuch acknowledged his need for guidance so that he might be able to gain understanding which motivated him to invite Philip to come and sit with him. The transitional purposes of God can lead us to those who require assistance in understanding the word of God.

The same Spirit that guides us into all truth (John 16:13) will use us to provide that same guidance to others. The divine connectivity that we have with God's Spirit will use us to connect to others so that the understanding that we have acquired about the Scriptures can be shared and provided.[281] The Ethiopian eunuch demonstrated a desire to receive the righteousness that is found in God's word (2 Timothy 3:16) and the Spirit used Philip to be the blessing that would satisfy the eunuch's hunger and his thirst (Matthew 5:6).

Jeffery Kirby considers the beatitudes provided in the Sermon on the Mount as a calling that spells out the path to holiness and happiness.[282] Once we have been blessed to have our own hunger and thirst satisfied, we should be ready and willing to be a blessing in return. Philip was blessed to have his hunger and thirst satisfied through the

---

[281] C. H. Sadaphal, "Connectivity: Acts 17," The Living Pulpit (Online) 24, no. 4 (Winter 2015): 14-16, accessed March 26, 2020, ATLA Religion Database with ATLASerials, EBSCOhost.

[282] Jeffery Kirby, "The Depth of the Beatitudes: Christ Spells Out the Path to Holiness, Happiness in Matthew 5," The Priest 75, no. 4 (Apr 2019): 43, accessed August 6, 2021, ATLA Religion Database with ATLASerials, EBSCOhost.

apostle's devotion to the ministry of the word (Acts 6:4) and the same devotion that was a blessing to Philp was used to allow him to be a blessing in return. Fulfilling the transitional purposes of God means taking advantage of the wisdom of those who are devoted to the ministry of word so that we might be used of the Spirit to be ministers of the word in return. God used Philip to fill in a gap for the Ethiopian eunuch that no one else around him was able to fill and so should it be with the followers of Jesus Christ.

In sum, ministerial opportunities for the majority of the followers of Jesus Christ will be filled with swift transitions. When transitions occur, there will be times when God may lead us to places where human perspective will be unable to perceive the possibility of success. Successful ministry should never be gauged by human perspective, but by obedience to what God has commanded. Since God has commanded that all nations should be taught to obey all that He has commanded, then the followers of Jesus Christ should be prepared to minister to those who are outside of their own ethnicity and culture.

Philip's ministry reveals that successful ministry should also not be gauged by quantity. Philip was transitioned out of a large ministry to a ministry of serving just one; one who held a higher status in life than Philip had gained for himself. God's transitional purposes may lead us to minister to those who have achieved a higher status in this life than our own; a purpose which should also draw us to the logical conclusion that ministry may also involve providing service to those of a lower status in this life than God has blessed us to achieve.

Fulfilling the transitional purposes of God will also mean providing and sharing the understanding of the word of God that we have acquired. The intention of the acquisition of understanding (Proverbs 4:7) is for the purpose of being a blessing to those who hunger and thirst for the understanding that the disciples of Christ have obtained.

CHAPTER TWELVE
FULFILLING GOD'S OPPORTUNISTIC PURPOSES

Acts 8:32-40 (ESV)

32Now the passage of the Scripture that he was reading was this: "Like a sheep he was led to the slaughter and like a lamb before its shearer is silent, so he opens not his mouth. 33In his humiliation justice was denied him. Who can describe his generation? For his life is taken away from the earth." 34And the eunuch said to Philip, "About whom, I ask you, does the prophet say this, about himself or about someone else?" 35Then Philip opened his mouth, and beginning with this Scripture he told him the good news about Jesus. 36 And as they were going along the road they came to some water, and the eunuch said, "See, here is water! What prevents me from being baptized?" 38 And he commanded the chariot to stop, and they both went down into the water, Philip and the eunuch, and he baptized him. 39 And when they came up out of the water, the Spirit of the Lord carried Philip away, and the eunuch saw him no more, and went on his way rejoicing. 40 But Philip found himself at Azotus, and as he passed through, he preached the gospel to all the towns until he came to Caesarea.

After Philip was commanded to go over and join the Ethiopian eunuch's chariot, no further commandment was provided to him. Once Philip heard the Ethiopian eunuch reading an excerpt from the prophet Isaiah, Philip understood the opportunity that God had placed before him. As followers of Jesus Christ, we should all have senses that have been so sharpened that we recognize the ministerial opportunities that God presents to us. Thiessen suggests that ministerial opportunities should be regularly included in our prayers.[283] But if we do not make the effort to sharpen our senses, then ministerial opportunities can easily be overlooked.

The Christian life has been identified as a race that has been set before us (Hebrews 12:1); a race that includes the good works that God prepared beforehand for us to do (Ephesians 2:10).[284] When the good works that God has prepared beforehand is set before us, then the response of the followers of Christ should be to immediately get to work.

Hebrews 12:1 additionally identifies the culprit that causes us to look past or even to ignore ministerial opportunities. The culprit is sin. The writer of Hebrews says that it weighs us down and clings to us. Proficiency in recognizing the ministerial opportunities that God sets before us increases as the weight of sin is laid aside. Scott D. Mackie notes that there are no specific sins identified in Hebrews 12:1 because all sin is a threat to the community of Christ followers.[285] If our senses are to be sharpened to the point where ministerial opportunities are no

---

[283] Jim Loepp Thiessen, " What's Stopping You? Philip and the Ethiopian Eunuch (Acts 8:25-39)," Vision (Winnipeg, Man) 4, no. 2 (Fall 2003): 54, accessed July 25, 2021, ATLA Religion Database with ATLASerials, EBSCOhost.

[284] "What Does It Mean to "Run the Race Set Before Us" (Hebrews 12:1)?" Got Questions: Your Questions: Biblical Answers, Got Questions Ministries, last updated April 26, 2021, https://www.gotquestions.org/run-the-race-set-before-us.html.

[285] Scott D. Mackie, "Visually Oriented Rhetoric and Visionary Experience in Hebrews 12:1-4," The Catholic Biblical Quarterly 79, no. 3 (Jul 2017): 492, accessed August 11, 2021, ATLA Religion Database with ATLASerials, EBSCOhost.

longer overlooked, then we need to be cleansed from sin; a cleansing which can only take place by living life consistently according to God's word (1 John 1:7).

Zane C. Hodges describes walking in the light (i.e., living according to God's word) as the only sphere where man can truly have communion with God.[286] It is within this sphere that the follower of Christ acknowledges whatever the light reveals is wrong in their life and they begin to walk contrary to the wrong so that they may be cleansed from it.[287] The more the blood of Jesus cleanses us from all sin, the clearer ministerial opportunities will become.

King David understood that if he was to be an effective teacher of the ways of God then he needed all of his transgressions to be blotted out (Psalm 51). If the followers of Christ are going to be both effective and opportunistic, then sin needs to be eradicated from their lives. 2 Timothy 2:21 insists that what makes us ready for every good work is when we cleanse ourselves from what is dishonorable so that we will be vessels for honorable use. The things that are dishonorable being clearly defined in 2 Timothy 2:19 as iniquity; that which contaminates the life of a follower of Christ.[288]

The ministerial opportunity that was set before Philip was to provide understanding to the Ethiopian eunuch. The Ethiopian eunuch had a specific question that was connected to a specific pericope of Scripture, Isaiah 53:7b-8c. Ellicott's Commentary for English Readers associates this particular pericope of Scripture with those that were appointed for use as lessons in the synagogue services.[289] Since the

---

[286] Zane C. Hodges, Bible Knowledge Commentary: An Exposition of the Scriptures by Dallas Seminary Faculty: New Testament Edition, ed. John F. Walvoord and Roy B. Zuck (Colorado Springs: ChariotVictor Publishing, 1983), 885.

[287] Ibid.

[288] A. Duane Litfin, Bible Knowledge Commentary: An Exposition of the Scriptures by Dallas Seminary Faculty: Old Testament, ed. John F. Walvoord and Roy B. Zuck (n.p.: SP Publications, 1985), 755.

[289] "Ellicott's Commentary for English Readers," Bible Hub, accessed August 11, 2021, https://biblehub.com/commentaries/ellicott/acts/8.htm

Ethiopian eunuch was returning from worship, then contextually it appears that the Ethiopian eunuch was looking for clarification that was not provided during the worship service. Like Philip, there may be ministerial opportunities to provide Scriptural clarifications that are not provided in worship.

In order to provide guidance to help the Corinthian church establish order in their worship services, the Apostle Paul gives the commandment for wives to make their inquiries at home (1 Corinthians 14:33-35); a rule that was made with special reference to time and circumstances.[290] The husband therefore is provided the ministerial opportunity to provide answers to his wife's inquiries. God's people should endeavor to be so familiar with the Scriptures that they may be able to provide answers to inquiries that are presented to them outside of the worship service.

It was from the misunderstood passage of Scripture that Philip began to tell the Ethiopian eunuch the good news about Jesus. Luke may be hinting at the methodology that is needed when taking advantage of the opportunity to provide understanding. Philip began with what was misunderstood. Psalm 119:130 provides that it is the unfolding of God's words that gives light and imparts understanding to the simple. What the Ethiopian eunuch needed was someone who could unfold Isaiah 53:7b-8c so that he might receive the light being imparted by those words. Ivana Procházková refers to Psalm 119:130 as the anchor for providing understanding.[291] The Ethiopian eunuch was groping for the light switch and God sent Philip to begin with the unfolding of Isaiah 53:7b-8c. As opportunistic followers of Christ who are sent to

---

[290.] "Pulpit Commentary," Bible Hub, accessed August 13, 2021, https://biblehub.com/commentaries/pulpit/1_corinthians/14.htm.

[291.] Ivana Procházková, "The Torah Within the Heart, In the Feet, and on the Tongue: Law and Freedom in Psalm 119 from the Perspective of Cognitive Linguistics," Communio viatorum 54, no. 1 (2012): 21, accessed August 22, 2021, ATLA Religion Database with ATLASerials, EBSCOhost.

provide understanding, the starting point should always be with what is misunderstood.

If Philip shared the good news of Jesus from the prophetic words of Isaiah 53:7b-8c, then it seems obvious that Philip began to elaborate on how Jesus was the fulfillment of those words. Even though the specific words of Philip are not provided, an educated hypothesis can be derived from the context of Isaiah 53:7b-8c in coordination with the Scriptures that describe their fulfillment.

Isaiah's prophecy speaks of how it was the arm of the Lord (Isaiah 53:1) who like a sheep was led to the slaughter and like a lamb before its shearer is silent. David Schrock identifies the arm of the Lord as a common metaphor used in Scripture to convey God's powerful actions within human history; a metaphor which is predominantly associated with the powerful actions of God in effecting salvation and deliverance for His people.[292] Schrock also derives from Scripture, how it was God who took on human form so that He might step into human history and become the arm of the Lord who would bring salvation to Himself.[293]

Isaiah 59:15-16 speaks of God seeing no man who could intercede for those who desired to depart from evil and therefore His own arm brought Him salvation. Arno Gaebelein insists that what moved Jehovah to intervene were those who desired to repent.[294] Salvation is only for those who desire to repent. God required someone in human flesh to be the intercessor between Himself and man, but there was no one who could answer the call (Isaiah 50:2). Therefore, being delighted to do God's will (Psalm 40:7-8), Christ came in the body that was prepared

---

[292] David Schrock, "The Arm of the Lord: From Moses to Isaiah to Christ," VIA EMMAUS, published December 13, 2017, https://davidschrock.com/2017/12/13/the-arm-of-the-lord-from-moses-to-isaiah-to-christ/.

[293] Schrock, Ibid.

[294] Arno Gaebelein, "Bible Commentaries: Arno Gaebelein's Annotated Bible: Isaiah 59," StudyLight.org, accessed August 29, 2021, https://www.studylight.org/commentaries/eng/gab/isaiah-59.html.

for Him (Hebrews 10:5) so that He might be the arm of the Lord that brought salvation.

Joseph was commanded by an angel of the Lord to call His name Jesus because He would save His people from their sins; the son who would be the fulfillment of the child who would be born of a virgin, but who would also be called Immanuel because this son would also be God with us (Matthew 1:20-23). Philip most likely shared that Jesus is the arm of the Lord who brought salvation.

Isaiah 53:7a prophesizes that the arm of the Lord would be oppressed and afflicted. Marc Brettler and Amy-Jill Levine believe that this refers to the terrible disabilities that the arm of the Lord would suffer; disabilities that would include having a physical appearance that would be marred beyond human semblance and having a form that would be beyond that of the children of mankind (Isaiah 52:14).[295] A servant who would be severely disabled and shunned.[296] The physical sufferings of Jesus included being bound as He was led from the garden of Gethsemane (John 18:12), scourged with a whip embedded with sheep bones and sharp pieces of metal (John 19:1), a crown of thorns rammed down on His head (Matthew 27:29), repeatedly being beaten with a mock scepter and spit upon (Mark 15:19), forced to carry a horizontal cross-beam through the streets (John 19:17), and of course being crucified on a cross resulting in death by suffocation (Mark 15:24, et al.).[297]

The sufferings of Jesus were more than just physical. The sufferings of Jesus included how He suffered emotionally and spiritually as well. The contextual passages of Isaiah 53:7b-8c foretell how the arm of the Lord would be despised and rejected by men (Isaiah 53:3). Emotionally Jesus suffered due to being slandered and being rejected by the religious leaders

---

[295.] Marc Brettler and Amy-Jill Levine, "Isaiah's Suffering Servant: Before and After Christianity," *Interpretation* 73, no. 2 (Apr 2019): 161, accessed August 31, 2021, ATLA Religion Database with ATLASerials, EBSCOhost.

[296.] Marc Brettler and Amy-Jill Levine, [161.]

[297.] Kevin Kleiman, "The Suffering of Jesus," Cities Church, last modified July 22, 2018, https://www.citieschurch.com/sermons/the-suffering-of-jesus.

(John 19:6, et al), government authorities (Matthew 27:26), and by His own disciples (Mark 14:50).[298] Spiritually He suffered due to feeling abandoned by God Himself (Matthew 27:46).[299] Philip most likely shared that Jesus is the arm of the Lord who was oppressed and afflicted.

Isaiah 53:7b, or even better yet, the Lukan rendering of Isaiah 53:7b (a rendering derived using Midrashic techniques and traditions where the fulfillment enlightens the promise) emphasizes that even though the arm of the Lord would be oppressed and afflicted, he would respond by being led like a sheep to the slaughter and like a lamb before its shearer is silent, so opening not his mouth.[300] Ellicott labels the opening not of his mouth as the silence of absolute acquiescence.[301] Jesus' prayed, "My Father, if it is not possible for this cup to be taken away unless I drink it, may your will be done" (Matthew 26:42 NIV). Jesus responded to Peter's attack on Malchus by stating, "Shall I not drink the cup that the Father has given Me?" The mindset of Jesus Christ was to fully acquiesce to the sufferings that had been predetermined for Him (Philippians 2: 5-8); acquiescence being an unconsidered virtue of what true divinity looks like.[302]

The Biblically reported events that actually describe Jesus not opening His mouth were during the times when false accusations were being made against Him (Matthew 26:59-63, et al.) and when the chief priests and officers insisted upon His crucifixion (John 19:4-9); portrayed in 1 Peter 2 as the silent sufferings of Christ.[303] Philip most likely shared that

---

[298] Ibid.

[299] Ibid.

[300] Paul B. Decock, "The Understanding of Isaiah 53:7-8 in Acts 8:32-33," Neotestamentica 14 (1981): 111, accessed September 3, 2021, ATLA Religion Database with ATLASerials, EBSCOhost.

[301] "Ellicott's Commentary for English Readers," Bible Hub, accessed August 29, 2021, https://biblehub.com/commentaries/ellicott/isaiah/53.htm.

[302] Hannah R. Stewart, "Self-emptying and Sacrifice: A Feminist Critique of Kenosis in Philippians 2," *Colloquium* 44, no. 1 (May 2012): 108, accessed September 5, 2021, ATLA Religion Database with ATLASerials, EBSCOhost.

[303] Marc Brettler and Amy-Jill Levine, 168.

Jesus is the arm of the Lord, who though oppressed and afflicted, suffered these things without opening His mouth.

The Lukan rendering of Isaiah 53:8a emphasizes the justice that would be denied to the one described as the arm of the Lord. The Hebrew rendering of Isaiah 53:8a expresses that by oppression and judgment the arm of the Lord would be taken away, but the Lukan rendering of Isaiah 53:8a which is influenced by its fulfillment expresses that in his humiliation justice would be denied him. The Gospels provide five witnesses that openly declared that Jesus was free from guilt. Pilate professed before the chief priests and the rulers that Jesus was innocent of the charges presented against Him and that Herod was in agreement (Luke 23:13-15). Pilate's wife sent word to Pilate to have nothing to do with this righteous man (Matthew 27:19). The thief who was crucified on the right of Jesus declared that though he himself deserved to die for his crimes, Jesus had not done anything wrong (Luke 23:41 NLT). Even Judas, the one who betrayed Jesus, acknowledged that he had betrayed innocent blood (Matthew 27:3-4). Philip most likely shared that Jesus is the arm of the Lord who was deprived of justice.

The question asked in the Lukan rendering of Isaiah 53:8b is who can describe his generation. Contextually, this question has to refer to a generation who would deprive justice. Decock informs us that the word generation can refer to a disobedient and a rebellious race of people.[304] Rather than fulfilling the call of God to seek and to bring justice (Isaiah 1:17), God's people had once again become a disobedient and rebellious race. Philip most likely shared that it was the generation that deprived Jesus due justice that had become an indescribable generation.

The pericope that the Ethiopian eunuch was reading concludes by contextually describing that it was the arm of the Lord whose life was taken from the earth (Isaiah 53:8c). The Masoretic text, which is considered to be the authoritative version of the Hebrew Bible, renders Isaiah

---

[304] Decock, 123.

53:8c with the words that he was cut off out of the land of the living.[305] Since the Lukan rendering is influenced by the fulfillment of the prophetic events, then Luke is referring to Jesus' death in spite of what others have suggested.[306] After being denied justice, Jesus was crucified on a cross where He breathed His last (Luke 23:46, et al). Philip most likely shared that it was Jesus whose life was taken from the earth.

Considering that the chapter pericope states that Philip only began to share the good news about Jesus from Isaiah 53:7b-8c, it is quite difficult to believe that Philip did not share that Jesus' death was a vicarious death; an atoning death that would make many accounted for righteousness because of His willingness to bear the sins of the many (Isaiah 53:11-12).[307] Philip most likely shared that it was Jesus who was pierced for our transgressions, crushed for our iniquities, chastised that it might bring us peace, and it is His wounds by which we are healed (Isaiah 53:5).

Sharing the good news of Jesus would be incomplete without the inclusion of His burial, His resurrection, and His appearances to many witnesses (1 Corinthians 15:3-8). Belief in the good news of Jesus Christ, in its completeness, is doctrinally considered to be the prerequisite for salvation (1 Corinthians 15:1-2).

Close examination of the chapter pericope reveals verse 37 missing from the ESV translation. Reason being, all manuscripts do not include the wording found in verse 37 which includes the Ethiopian eunuch's confession of faith that he believed that Jesus Christ is the Son of God.[308] If Acts 8:37 is appraised as being a proper inclusion, then the consideration that Philip shared the good news of Jesus in its completeness is not farfetched.

---

[305] The Jewish Publication Society of America, *The Holy Scriptures According to the Masoretic Text; A New Translation* (Chicago: The Lakeside Press 1917).

[306] Marc Brettler and Amy-Jill Levine, [160].

[307] Marc Brettler and Amy-Jill Levine, [162].

[308] "Acts 8: English Standard Version: footnote e," BibleGateway, accessed September 8, 2021, https://www.biblegateway.com/passage/?search=Acts+8&version=ESV.

The context of the Isaiah 53:7b-8c speaks of the arm of the Lord having an assigned grave with the wicked and with the rich in his death (Isaiah 53:9 NIV). Jesus' grave assignment was intended to be with the two criminals with whom He was crucified had it not been for the interference of a rich man by the name of Joseph of Arimathea, who took the body of Jesus and laid it in his own new tomb (Matthew 27:38, 57).[309] Herald Gandi describes that burial is the confirmation of death.[310]

Isaiah 53:10 speaks of the prolonging of the days of the arm of the Lord. The verb "prolong" is sometimes used to refer to an everlasting afterlife and portrays the resurrection of the one called the arm of the Lord.[311] Though Jesus was delivered into the hands of sinful men and was crucified, on the third day Jesus rose again (Luke 24:1-7). The Davidic Covenant fails if the Messiah is not resurrected from the dead (cf. 2 Samuel 7:12-13).[312]

Isaiah 53:10 moreover provides the prophetic words that the arm of Lord shall see his offspring. The verb "see" in this context is not only referred to as the ability to gaze or to look at, but it also refers to the ability to be seen or to present oneself.[313] Therefore, the prophecy suggests that not only would the arm of the Lord see his offspring, but his offspring would also see him because he would present himself to them. All four Gospel writers as well as the book of Acts record the resurrection appearances of Jesus Christ (Luke 24, et al.); appearances which were to those who were appointed beforehand by God (Acts 10:41 HCSB) and totaled to be in excess of over five hundred (1 Corinthians 15:5-8). Philip most

---

[309] "Pulpit Commentary," Bible Hub, accessed September 8, 2021, https://biblehub.com/commentaries/pulpit/isaiah/53.htm.

[310] Herald Gandi, "The Resurrection: "According to the Scriptures"?" The Master's Seminary Blog, July 31, 2018, https://blog.tms.edu/resurrection-according-to-scriptures.

[311] Ibid.

[312] Ibid.

[313] "H7200 – rā'â – Outline of Biblical Usage," Blue Letter Bible, accessed September 12, 2021, https://www.blueletterbible.org/lexicon/h7200/esv/wlc/0-1/.

likely shared that not only was Jesus buried as confirmation of His death, but that He also rose on the third day and appeared to many who served as witnesses to Jesus' resurrection.

The Ethiopian eunuch's response to the good news that Philip shared with him may also provide a clue to what additionally may have been included in what needed to be understood. The eunuch responded, "See, here is water! What prevents me from being baptized?"; noted by various scholars as a response of eagerness and excitement.[314] For the eunuch to make the observation about the presence of water and ask the question what prevents me from being baptized, the subject of baptism must have been broached.

During one of Christ's resurrection appearances, Jesus said that in conjunction with His suffering and being raised on the third day, repentance for the forgiveness of sins should be proclaimed in His name to all nations (Luke 24:46-47). Peter, in obedience to what Christ had commanded, answered those who became distraught after hearing his message on the day of Pentecost that they needed to repent and be baptized in the name of Jesus Christ for the forgiveness of their sins (Acts 2:37-38). For the Ethiopian eunuch to make the observation about the presence of water and to ask the question what prevents me from being baptized, Philip most likely shared the same message of repentance and the need to be baptized.[315]

The Ethiopian eunuch's desire to be baptized resulted in a command for the chariot to be brought to a halt. The Ethiopian eunuch's command provides the revelation that there were others in ear shot of the good news of Jesus being shared with the eunuch. Philip was also scattering the seed of God's word in some unintentional places. As followers of Jesus Christ, when we take full advantage of ministerial opportunities to

---

[314.] Heather M. Gorman, "Stone-Campbell Interpretations of the Ethiopian Eunuch (Acts 8:26-40): Observations on the Last 50 Years," *Stone-Campbell Journal* 23, no. 1 (Spr 2020): 13, accessed September 14, 2021, ATLA Religion Database with ATLASerials, EBSCOhost.

[315.] Ibid., 9.

provide understanding to those who pursue it, the understanding that is shared may also have the opportunity to fall on the ears of those to whom it was not intentionally directed.

Isaiah 55:11 distinctly expresses that God's word does not return empty, but it accomplishes that which He has purposed. Though the word that we share may fall on unintended ears, God is well aware of the presence of the unintended and His word will accomplish the purpose intended for them as well. Gerard Bernard and Dan Lioy denote that Isaiah 55:11 is located within a passage that highlights the theme of repentance.[316] It is highly possible that God was not only using Philip to preach repentance to the Ethiopian eunuch, but He also may have been using Philip to preach repentance to the unintended as well.

When the Apostle Paul told Timothy to be persistent in sharing the word of God so that he might save himself and his hearers, he probably never considered that there might be hearers who were unintended (1 Timothy 4:16). The opportunistic followers of Jesus Christ should remain persistent in hopes that even unintentional hearers might be saved by the understanding of the word being shared.

Scholarly discussions about the Ethiopian eunuch's baptism seem to find their focus on the mode of baptism. Some argue that the mode of baptism was immersion, while others insist that Luke does not indicate the mode of baptism.[317] The aspect of the eunuch's baptism that seems to be overlooked is its sincerity.

The Ethiopian eunuch was not prodded by Philip into being baptized, the eunuch willingly responded to the good news of Jesus that was shared with him.[318] This man of great authority was willing to surrender his life to the authority of Christ in the presence of those over which he held

---

[316] Gerard Bernard and Dan Lioy, "Isaiah 55:11 with New Creation Theme and the Servant of the Lord as Witnessed in Jesus in the Fourth Gospel," *Conspectus* 29, (Mar 2020): 27, accessed September 15, 2021, ATLA Religion Database with ATLASerials, EBSCOhost.

[317] Gorman, 10-11.

[318] Thiessen, 55.

authority. This man refused to allow prestige and position from keeping him from taking advantage of the immediate opportunity to be baptized. The Ethiopian eunuch humbled himself so that he might be exalted to become a citizen of the kingdom of God and so that God would be glorified in the presence of those who were subordinate to him. As followers of Jesus Christ, we should be ever so willing to take advantage of the opportunity to humble ourselves to the authority of Christ so that God may be glorified in the presence of those who may be subordinate to us.

The Ethiopian eunuch's baptism became a time of rejoicing for him. But God did not allow Philip to participate in the eunuch's time of rejoicing, because the Spirit of the Lord carried Philip away. Philip being carried away did not seem to hinder the eunuch's time of rejoicing nor does it appear that his rejoicing was hindered because he rejoiced alone. The Ethiopian eunuch's faith response to the new-found truth of Jesus Christ resulted in joy that prevailed regardless to the circumstances that currently surrounded him.[319] This may be Luke's rhetorical method of indicating that the Ethiopian eunuch had been endowed with the presence of God's Spirit (Romans 15:13).

The chapter pericope closes by identifying that Philip had been carried away to Azotus. Easton's Bible Dictionary suggests that Azotus is the Grecized form of Ashdod; one of the five chief cities of the Philistines.[320] Luke identifies that Philip's travels took him from Azotus to Caesarea, a city named by Herod the Great after the Roman emperor Augustus Caesar.[321] Ministerially, Luke infers that no matter where Philip found himself, his mission remained the same. He continued to preach the gospel no matter where he found himself. As opportunistic followers of

---

[319] "Acts 8: Ellicott's Commentary for English Readers," Ibid.

[320] "Definitions: The Meaning of Azotus in the Bible," BIBLETOOLS, accessed September 17, 2021, https://www.bibletools.org/index.cfm/fuseaction/Def.show/RTD/Easton/ID/379/Azotus.htm.

[321] "Philip's Journeys," The Bible Journey, accessed September 17, 2021, https://www.thebiblejourney.org/biblejourney1/7-journeys-of-jesuss-followers/philips-journeys/.

Jesus Christ, we should always be willing to preach the good news of Jesus no matter where we might find ourselves.

In summary, Philip's recognition of the ministerial opportunity that God had placed before him and his willingness to take full advantage of the opportunity is what ultimately led to the Ethiopian eunuch taking advantage of his opportunity to be baptized for the forgiveness of his sins. No matter where the Spirit led Philip, he continued to take advantage of the opportunity to preach Jesus wherever his travels took him. Every follower of Jesus Christ should demonstrate the same zealousness as it relates to ministerial opportunities because it might also lead to some inquisitive soul expressing their desire to be baptized for the forgiveness of their sins.

CHAPTER THIRTEEN
Fulfilling God's Transformative Purposes

Acts 21:8-14 (ESV)

⁸ On the next day we departed and came to Caesarea, and we entered the house of Philip the evangelist, who was one of the seven, and stayed with him. ⁹ He had four unmarried daughters, who prophesied. ¹⁰ While we were staying for many days, a prophet named Agabus came down from Judea. ¹¹ And coming to us, he took Paul's belt and bound his own feet and hands and said, "Thus says the Holy Spirit, 'This is how the Jews at Jerusalem will bind the man who owns this belt and deliver him into the hands of the Gentiles.'" ¹² When we heard this, we and the people there urged him not to go up to Jerusalem. ¹³ Then Paul answered, "What are you doing, weeping and breaking my heart? For I am ready not only to be imprisoned but even to die in Jerusalem for the name of the Lord Jesus." ¹⁴ And since he would not be persuaded, we ceased and said, "Let the will of the Lord be done."

Luke's compilation of Philip's journey of fulfilling God's purposes for his life conclude with Philip finding what seems to be a permanent residence in Caesarea. Philip's absolute surrender to the guidance and the leadership of the Holy Spirit led him from Jerusalem to Samaria, from Samaria to a desert road, from a desert road to the city of Azotus, and from the city of Azotus to the city of Caesarea; Caesarea being the place chosen by Luke to conclude his biographical depiction of the life of Philip. [322]

The King James translation of Acts 21:8 includes that those who had come to Caesarea were those who were of Paul's company. The Apostle Paul was now on his third missionary journey and was being accompanied by eight companions.[323] Acts 20:4-6 names Paul's companions as Sopater the Berean, Aristarchus and Secundus of Thessalonica, Gaius and Timothy of Derbe, Tychicus and Trophimus of Asia, along with Luke as well. God saw fit to allow the journeys of the Apostle Paul and Philip to cross paths in the city that Philip now called home.

Luke identifies Philip as the evangelist, a herald of salvation through Christ; a label that encapsulated what Philip had become through the transformative purposes of God.[324] Philip had been given as a gift from God to everyone that he encountered along his Christian journey so that others might have the opportunity to hear the good news of Jesus Christ (Ephesians 4:11-13). As followers of Jesus Christ, we should allow ourselves to become gifts that God has given to others to serve His purposes and to be a blessing to others; a transformation that occurs as we surrender ourselves to the leadership and the guidance of God's Holy Spirit.

The Apostle Peter admonishes us to be good stewards of God's manifold grace which is accomplished by using whatever gift we have

---

[322.] "Philip's Journeys," The Bible Journey, accessed September 17, 2021, https://www.thebiblejourney.org/biblejourney1/7-journeys-of-jesuss-followers/philips-journeys/.

[323.] "Apostle Paul Life, Teaching & Theology: The Companions of Paul & Biblical Persons Related to Paul," Christian Pilgrimage Journeys, accessed September 28, 2021, https://www.christian-pilgrimage-journeys.com/biblical-sources/apostle-paul-life-teaching-theology/companions-of-paul/.

[324.] "G2099 – *euangelistēs* – Outline of Biblical Usage," Blue Letter Bible, accessed October 6, 2021, https://www.blueletterbible.org/lexicon/g2099/kjv/tr/0-1/.

Fulfilling God's Transformative Purposes

received to serve one another; a service that flows from our deep love for one another. It is through the use of our gifts in order to serve one another that God is glorified through our Lord, Jesus Christ (1 Peter 4:8-11 BSB). As recipients of God's grace, we become manifesters of His grace by using our gifts to serve one another.[325] The use of our gifts to serve one another is evidence that God's transformative purposes are at work with in us.

Not only does Luke use this pericope to encapsulate what Philip had become, but Luke also reminds us that Philp was also one of the seven; a reminder that rhetorically connects Philip from what he was to what he had become. Becoming the evangelist was the consequence of Philip remaining consistently obedient to the Spirit of Christ. Philip did not begin as the evangelist, but the evangelist is what he became through the transformative purposes of God. Transformation connects the followers of Christ from what they were to what God would have them to become through their vigilant obedience to the leadership and guidance of God's Spirit.

Philip did not possess the detailed foreknowledge of what he would become, only the foreknowledge of what God expected at each phase of his journey and being obedient to it. Philip trusted the plan of God to transform him into what he would become. Having the detailed foreknowledge of what God would have us to become is not a prerequisite to becoming what God would have us to become, only the foreknowledge of what God expects of us at each phase of our journey and being obedient to it. Detailed foreknowledge is best left in the hands of God.

Some might even argue that having detailed knowledge of what God would have us to become is more harmful than helpful. Moses supposed that the Israelites understood that God was giving them salvation by his hand (Acts 7:25), but this foreknowledge led to Moses doing what seemed right rather than waiting on God to reveal how the Israelites'

[325.] Roger M. Raymer, *Bible Knowledge Commentary: An Exposition of the Scriptures by Dallas Seminary Faculty: New Testament Edition*, ed. John F. Walvoord and Roy B. Zuck (Colorado Springs: ChariotVictor Publishing, 1983), 855.

salvation would be achieved through him; actions that proved themselves to be noble, but at the same time foolish.[326] This foreknowledge resulted in Moses' failure to seek God about what he should do or when he should do it.[327] If the followers of Jesus Christ desire to fulfill their transformative purposes by becoming what God would have them to become, then the only prerequisites are to trust God and to be remain obedient at every phase of their Christian journey.

Philip was not only willing to use his spiritual gifts to be a blessing to others, but Philip was also willing to use his worldly goods. Philip allowed Paul and the entirety of his company to stay with him for many days; many days being an inference of the extent of Philip's generosity. These were nine adult men that needed to be housed and fed, but Philip was willing to be a blessing to them all. On this Christian journey, God not only expects for us to use our spiritual gifts to be a blessing, but God also expects for us to be a blessing through our willingness to share those things which He has allowed us to possess.

2 Corinthians 9:11 furnishes that God enriches us in every way so that we might also be generous in every way; a good work that is done through the enablement of God.[328] Whenever God enriches us in any way, that enrichment provides the opportunity to be generous to others. The Apostle Paul designates the generosity that is extended out of the enrichments that are given by God as a ministry of service to the saints (1 Corinthians 9:12); charitable gestures that demonstrate the sincerity of one's confession and the vitality of their spiritual lives.[329] The trans-

---

[326.] John W. Ritenbaugh, "Commentaries: Forerunner Commentary – Acts 7:24-25," BIBLETOOLS, accessed October 8, 2021, https://www.bibletools.org/index.cfm/fuseaction/Bible.show/sVerseID/27142/eVerseID/27142.

[327.] Ibid.

[328.] David K. Lowery, *Bible Knowledge Commentary: An Exposition of the Scriptures by Dallas Seminary Faculty: New Testament Edition*, ed. John F. Walvoord and Roy B. Zuck (Colorado Springs: ChariotVictor Publishing, 1983), 575.

[329.] Ibid.

formative purposes of God are being fulfilled in the lives of those who live to glorify Christ through generosities that are shared with others.

Luke makes no mention of Philip having or even that he once had a wife, only that he had four daughters. Luke impresses upon us, either intentionally or unintentionally, the amount of time that had passed in the life of Philip the evangelist. Philip has been in Caesarea long enough for God to have blessed him with a home and four daughters.

Scripture provides that a similar occurrence transpired in the lives of the midwives, Shiphrah and Puah. They were blessed as well with families of their own (translated as households in various translations) because their actions were motivated by their fear of God more than their fear of man (Exodus 1:15-21).[330] As stated previously in chapter three of this writing project, the Jewish hermeneutical device, gezerah shawah, allows for implied applicability due to contextual similarities.[331] Maybe Luke's implication is that even though Philip had been in Caesarea for quite some time at this juncture of his life, his actions were still motivated by his fear of God. The transformative purposes of God are fulfilled when our actions are motivated out of our fear for God. When our actions are motivated out of our fear of God, then we open ourselves up to receive the blessings of God.

Luke does more than just identify that Philip had four daughters, but that he had four daughters that prophesied. Luke's rhetorical intent may have been to draw attention to the fulfillment of Joel's prophetic statement which was also quoted by the Apostle Peter in his message on the day of Pentecost (Joel 2:28, Acts 2:17).[332] Not only was Joel's prophecy fulfilled on the day of Pentecost, but we also see its prophetic

---

[330] "Exodus 1:21," Bible Hub, accessed October 12, 2021, https://biblehub.com/exodus/1-21.htm.

[331] Richard B. Hays, *Echoes of Scripture in the Letters of Paul* (New Haven: Yale University Press, 1989): 13.

[332] Devin White, "Confronting Oracular Contradiction in Acts 21:1-14," *Novum Testamentum* 58, no. 1 (2016): 34, accessed October 10, 2021, ATLA Religion Database with ATLASerials, EBSCOhost.

fulfillment in the lives of Philip's daughters. The same Spirit that filled Philip had been poured out on his daughters evidenced by their ability to prophecy. Philip not only had an impact on those whom he encountered as a traveling evangelist, but apparently, he also had an impact on those who were of his own household. For those of us who are trusting God to fulfill His transformative purposes in our own lives, not only should our lives have an influence upon those who we encounter outside of the home but we should also have an influence on those who are of our own household.

Charles Haddon Spurgeon insists that God, by means of one of a household, draws the rest to Himself.[333] After Andrew began to follow Jesus, he first found his own brother, Simon Peter, so that he might influence him with the good news of the Messiah (John 1:40-41). Just like Andrew, one of our first pursuits should be to have an influence upon those who are of our own household. Though the results of our influence may not pan out as we might hope, it should give us a peace in knowing that we have done all that we could to lead those of our own household to Christ.

The remaining descriptive associated with Philip's daughters is that they were unmarried. Philip's daughters were free to exercise their gift unimpeded by the restrictions of marriage (1 Corinthians 7:34). Margaret Minnicks comments that the unmarried have the freedom to serve God unencumbered and can develop a deep relationship with God because they have fewer distractions.[334] For the followers of Jesus Christ who are untethered to the responsibilities of marriage, they should consider this a time of freedom to exercise their gift. For however long God's transformative purpose for the follower of Christ is to

---

[333.] Charles Haddon Spurgeon, "Household Salvation," The Spurgeon Center for Biblical Preaching at Midwestern Seminary, accessed October 20, 2021, https://www.spurgeon.org/resource-library/sermons/household-salvation/#flipbook/.

[334.] Margaret Minnicks, "Singleness: What the Bible Says About Being Single," PairedLife, accessed October 13, 2021, https://pairedlife.com/single-life/Singleness-What-the-Bible-Says-about-Being-Single.

be unmarried, then it should be considered an honor to follow in the footsteps of the unmarried faithful who lived their lives completely devoted to the service of God; there being none greater than Jesus Christ Himself.

The prophet Agabus is also described as someone who was sent on a journey. His journey was to travel from Judea down to Caesarea. Under the influence of the Holy Spirit, Agabus was sent to the home of Philip in Caesarea to foretell what would happen to Paul in Jerusalem; how he would be bound and delivered into the hands of the Gentiles. Agabus' predictive oracle was obviously given credence based on the response of those who heard his words; they urged Paul not to go to Jerusalem.[335]

Luke reports in Acts 11:27-28 that Agabus foretold of a great famine that would occur over all the world; a predictive oracle that came to pass. It was through this fulfilled predictive oracle that Agabus proved himself to be a true prophet who did indeed speak in the name of the Lord (Deuteronomy 18:21-22). Agabus was known as a prophet who spoke words that carried credence. Though a follower of Jesus Christ may not carry the title of a prophet, we should still speak words that carry credence.

For those of us who have submitted ourselves to the transformative purposes of God, we are being sanctified in the word of truth (John 17:17) and as those who are being sanctified in the word of truth, we have been commanded to speak the truth (Ephesians 4:15, 25); a practical result for those who are in a redeemed and learning relationship with Christ.[336] When we speak the truth, especially the truths that are found in God's word, then the words that we speak will be the most credible words that anyone is able to speak.

The urgings for Paul not to go to Jerusalem were also accompanied by weeping. Paul responded to their urgings and their tears by declaring

---

[335.] White, 36.

[336.] Mark Stirling, "Transformed Walking and Missional Temple Building: Discipleship in Ephesians," *Presbyterion* 45, no. 2 (Fall 2019): 92, accessed October 15, 2021, ATLA Religion Database with ATLASerials, EBSCOhost.

that they were breaking his heart and that he was ready not only to be imprisoned but to die for the name of the Lord Jesus. This response by Paul hints at the transformative purposes of God being at work in his life. This same Paul (the Greek form of the Hebrew name Saul) who once bound and imprisoned those who called upon the name of the Lord so that they might be put to death (Acts 9:2-21; 22:4-5) was now ready for the exact same fate to befall him, especially since it aligned with the Lord's will for him.[337] With the same zeal that Paul used as a persecutor of the church (Philippians 3:6), he was now willing to use as a submissive servant of the church to submit himself to the Lord's will being done in his life. For those of us who desire that the transformative purposes of God be fulfilled in our own lives, we should be just as zealous when it comes to the Lord's will being done as we did when we were willful participants in ungodliness.

The prophetic words of Isaiah about the first coming of the Lord states that He would wrap Himself in zeal as a cloak (Isaiah 59:17). It was with zealousness that the Lord secured our salvation.[338] If it was with zealousness that the Lord secured our salvation, then it should be with zealousness that we surrender to the Lord's will being done in every phase of our lives so that God's transformative purposes will be fulfilled throughout our lives. We have been predestined to be conformed to the image of God's Son (Romans 8:29) and that image includes a zealousness for the Lord's will being done.

Once Philip and the men of Paul's company realized that Paul would not be persuaded against going to Jerusalem, Luke tells us that the urgings and the tears ceased and they all acknowledged that the Lord's will should be done. While the transformative purposes of God are being fulfilled in our lives, emotional moments will transpire. But

---

[337.] "Who was Saul of Tarsus in the Bible?" CompellingTruth, accessed October 15, 2021, https://www.compellingtruth.org/Saul-of-Tarsus.html.

[338.] Albert Barnes, "Bible Commentaries: Albert Barnes' Notes on the Whole Bible: Isaiah 59," Studylight.org, accessed October 15, 2021, https://www.studylight.org/commentaries/eng/bnb/isaiah-59.html#verse-17.

as followers of Jesus Christ, we should not allow emotional moments to have a greater influence over us than surrendering to the Lord's will being done. Jesus confessed to Peter, James, and John that His soul was very sorrowful over what He was about to go through as He headed for the cross, but He would not let His emotions be a greater influence than what the Lord's will was for Him (Matthew 26:36-42). And just like Jesus, emotions should take a back seat to the Lord's will being done.

In summary, as followers of Jesus Christ, we should willfully and joyfully surrender ourselves to the leadership and the guidance of the Holy Spirit so that we may be transformed into what God has preordained; a transformation that aligns with the plan that God has for our lives (Jeremiah 29:11) and is actualized through our obedience throughout every phase of our Christian journey. Foreknowledge of what God would have us to become is not a prerequisite. The only prerequisites are the fear of God, trust in God, and complete allegiance to God.

CONCLUSION
Chapter Summarizations

Philip's purpose filled journey began with fulfilling God's societal purposes as a citizen of the kingdom of Jesus Christ; a purpose that is fulfilled through an undaunting allegiance to Jesus Christ as King and complete loyalty to all that He has commanded (Chapter One).[339] As a loyal citizen of the kingdom of Christ, Philip was impacted by the positive influences that touched his life; others who had also been impacted by the outpouring of God's Spirit (Chapter Two).[340] Philip demonstrated, along with the entirety of the community of disciples, great pleasure when a Biblical solution was provided to the dilemma that they were facing; a solution that was born out of the study of God's word and then shared with the disciples (Chapter Three).[341] What should stir up pleasure in the followers of Christ is the opportunity to please God through the applicability of what has been divinely inspired in His word.

[339.] Matthew W. Bates, *Salvation by Allegiance Alone: Rethinking Faith, Works, and the Gospel of Jesus the King* (Grand Rapids: Baker Academic, 2017), chap. 9, Kindle.

[340.] Craig S. Keener, *The IVP Bible Background Commentary New Testament*, (Downers Grove: Intervarsity Press, 1993), 330.

[341.] John W. Ritenbaugh, "Commentaries: Forerunner Commentary – Colossians 1:9-11," BIBLETOOLS, accessed June 18, 2020, https://www.bibletools.org/index.cfm/fuseaction/Bible.show/sVerseID/29475/eVerseID/29475.

As one of the seven, Philip was ministerially attached to Stephen who has been characterized as the model laymen.[342] Stephen demonstrated himself to be an exemplary disciple of Jesus Christ; an example of the type of attachments that should inspire the followers of Jesus Christ to become exemplary themselves (Chapter Four). As an exemplary example for Philip, Stephen evidenced how to verbally respond to false accusations while maintaining gentleness and respect; responses that reflect the hope that lies within us, but are also responses that actively seek peace even in the context of potentially abusive situations (Chapter Five).[343] Stephen's exemplary example continued to persist, though his respectful responses to his false accusers were met with hostility. Stephen's reaction completely contrasted the hostility that was directed towards him; the same radical reaction that should be emulated by all those who are under the continual influence of the Holy Spirit (Chapter Six).[344]

The hostility aimed at Stephen ultimately extended to hostilities being directed at the church; scattering them to the surrounding regions. God allowed this time of hostility as a motivator to entice the church to fulfill the great commission; the commission that extends to every follower of Jesus Christ (Chapter Seven).[345] The scattering resulted in Philip being specifically led to the city of Samaria with a very specific message, Philip preached to them the Christ. Philip's distinct intention

---

[342] Charles Harris Nash, "Stephen, the Model Layman: The Unique, Transcendent Image of Jesus in Life and Death, 'Filled with all the Fulness of God.' Acts 6-7," *Review & Expositor* 23, no. 4 (Oct 1926): 452, accessed September 15, 2020, ATLA Religion Database with ATLASerials, EBSCOhost.

[343] James B. Prothro, "Distance, Tolerance, and Honor: Six Theses on Romans 13:1-7," *Concordia Journal* 42, no. 4 (Fall 2016): 294, accessed October 30, 2020, ATLA Religion Database with ATLASerials, EBSCOhost.

[344] Piotr Nyk, "You are Witnesses of These Things! (Luke 24:48): The Concept of Testimony in the Gospel of Luke," *Verbum Vitae* 27, (2015): 121, accessed December 23, 2020, ATLA Religion Database with ATLASerials, EBSCOhost.

[345] Kolawole Olumafemi Paul, "The Great Commission Mandate of the Church in Matthew 28:18-20," *Word & World* 40, no. 4 (Fall 2020): 424, accessed February 17, 2021, ATLA Religion Database with ATLASerials, EBSCOhost.

through the use of his God given gifts and his proclamations of the Christ was to ensure that Christ was glorified; a distinctive that should characterize all Christ followers (Chapter Eight).[346] While in Samaria, God juxtaposed Philip against a sorcerer named Simon whose only aspiration was to glorify himself. God used this juxtaposing to draw others to salvation; a purpose for which God desires to be fulfilled by all His children (Chapter Nine).[347]

Philip fulfills the deferential purposes of God when Peter and John arrive in Samaria; a demonstration of the honor and respect that Philip held for the Apostles.[348] Philip's deferment to Peter and John was not only a demonstration of the honor and respect that he had for them, but it also allowed Peter and John to be used of God as well (Chapter Ten). The Spirit saw fit to transition Philip out of his successful ministry in the city of Samaria to a desert road that led from Jerusalem to Gaza where he was used of God to provide understanding for an Ethiopian eunuch. This Spirit mandated transition resulted in salvation in an unlikely place; an event that was precipitated by Philip's trust in the leadership and the guidance of God (Chapter Eleven).[349] Philip took full advantage of this opportunity for ministry by extending himself to the Ethiopian eunuch to provide the understanding that the eunuch was seeking; a characteristic that should be exuded by every opportunistic follower of Jesus Christ (Chapter Twelve).

---

[346] Donald H. Juel, "Hearing Peter's Speech in Acts 3: Meaning and Truth in Interpretation," *Word & Word* 12, no. 1 (Wint 1992): 45, accessed May 13, 2021, ATLA Religion Database with ATLASerials, EBSCOhost.

[347] "What Does It Mean that God Draws Us to Salvation?" Got Questions: Your Questions: Biblical Answers, Got Questions Ministries, last updated April 26, 2021, https://www.gotquestions.org/drawn-salvation.html.

[348] "What Does 1 Timothy 5:17 Mean?" BibleRef.com, accessed July 1, 2021, https://www.bibleref.com/1-Timothy/5/1-Timothy-5-17.html#commentary.

[349] Norman C. Habel, "Symbolism of Wisdom in Proverbs 1-9," *Interpretation* 26, no. 2 (Apr 1972): 146, accessed July 25, 2021, ATLA Religion Database with ATLASerials, EBSCOhost.

The concluding chapter on the biographic of Philip provides the summarization of what Philip had become through the transformative purposes of God. Philip became known as the evangelist, a herald of salvation through Christ.[350] As followers of Christ, the transformative purposes of God are fulfilled in our own lives as we surrender ourselves to the leadership and the guidance of God's Holy Spirit (Chapter Thirteen). An examination of the life of Philip clarifies that the call of God is not the fulfillment of one singular purpose, but the fulfillment of the purposes that present themselves at any given time along the Christian journey.

[350.] "G2099 – *euangelistēs* – Outline of Biblical Usage," Blue Letter Bible, accessed October 6, 2021, https://www.blueletterbible.org/lexicon/g2099/kjv/tr/0-1/.

Bibliography

"907. baptizō: Strong's Concordance." Bible Hub. Accessed June 22, 2021. https://biblehub.com/greek/907.htm.

"2840. koinoó: Strong's Concordance." Bible Hub. Accessed July 30, 2021. https://biblehub.com/greek/2840.htm.

"Acts 8: English Standard Version: footnote e." BibleGateway. Accessed September 8, 2021. https://www.biblegateway.com/passage/?search=Acts+8&version=ESV.

"Acts 8:9." Bible Hub. Accessed June 8, 2021. https://biblehub.com/acts/8-9.htm.

Amzallag, Gérard Nissim. "Psalm 67 and the Cosmopolite Musical Worship of YHWH." *Bulletin for Biblical Research* 25, no. 2 (2015): 172. Accessed July 30, 2021. ATLA Religion Database with ATLASerials, EBSCOhost.

"Apostle Paul Life, Teaching & Theology: The Companions of Paul & Biblical Persons Related to Paul." Christian Pilgrimage Journeys. Accessed September 28, 2021. https://www.christian-pilgrimage-journeys.com/biblical-sources/apostle-paul-life-teaching-theology/companions-of-paul/.

Apple, Raymond. "The Happy Man of Psalms 1." *Jewish Bible Quarterly* 40, no. 3 (Jul-Sep 2012): 180-181. Accessed July 3, 2020. ATLA Religion Database with ATLASerials, EBSCOhost.

Aquinas, Thomas. "Patristic Bible Commentary: St. Thomas Aquinas on 2 Corinthians: Chapter 5." Accessed August 31, 2020. https://sites.google.com/site/aquinasstudybible/home/2-corinthians/

st-thomas-aquinas-on-2-corinthians/chapter-1/chapter-2/chapter-3/chapter-4/chapter-5.

———. "Patristic Bible Commentary: St. Thomas Aquinas on Galatians: Chapter 5." sites.google.com. Accessed June 13, 2021, https://sites.google.com/site/aquinasstudybible/home/galatians/st-thomas-aquinas-on-galatians/chapter-1/chapter-2/chapter-3/chapter-4/chapter-5.

Ballenger, Isam E. "Ephesians 4:1-16." *Interpretation* 51, no. 3 (Jul 1997): 292-293. Accessed April 7, 2020. ATLA Religion Database with ATLASerials, EBSCOhost.

Barnes, Albert. "Bible Commentaries: Albert Barnes' Notes on the Whole Bible: 1 Peter 5." Studylight.org. Accessed May 20, 2020. https://www.studylight.org/commentaries/bnb/1-peter-5.html#3.

———. "Bible Commentaries: Albert Barnes' Notes on the Whole Bible: Isaiah 59." Studylight.org. Accessed October 15, 2021. https://www.studylight.org/commentaries/eng/bnb/isaiah-59.html#verse-17.

Bartling, Walter J. "The Congregation of Christ – A Charismatic Body: An Exegetical Study of 1 Corinthians 12." *Concordia Theological Monthly* 40, no. 2 (Feb 1969): 67, 69. Accessed July 14, 2020. ATLA Religion Database with ATLASerials, EBSCOhost.

Bates, Matthew W. *Salvation by Allegiance Alone: Rethinking Faith, Works, and the Gospel of Jesus the King.* Grand Rapids: Baker Academic, 2017. Kindle.

Beale, G. K., ed. *The Right Doctrine from the Wrong Texts? Essays on the Use of the Old Testament in the New.* Grand Rapids: Baker Academics 1994.

Bechard, Dean Philip. "Paul Among the Rustics: The Lystran Episode (Acts 14:8-20) and Lucan Apologetic." *The Catholic Biblical Quarterly* 63, no. 1 (Jan 2001): 96. Accessed June 16, 2021. ATLA Religion Database with ATLASerials, EBSCOhost.

Bibliography

Behr, John. "Colossians 1:13-20: A Chiastic Reading." *St. Vladimir's Theological Quarterly* 40, no.4 (1996): 250. Accessed April 14, 2020. ATLA Religion Database with ATLASerials, EBSCOhost.

Bernard, Gerard, and Dan Lioy. "Isaiah 55:11 with New Creation Theme and the Servant of the Lord as Witnessed in Jesus in the Fourth Gospel." *Conspectus* 29, (Mar 2020): 27. Accessed September 15, 2021. ATLA Religion Database with ATLASerials, EBSCOhost.

Bengel, Johann. "Bengel's Gnomon of the New Testament." Biblehub.com. Accessed April 4, 2021. https://biblehub.com/commentaries/bengel/1_corinthians/16.htm.

Berg, Shane. "Ben Sira, the Genesis Creation Accounts, and the Knowledge of God's Will." *Journal of Biblical Literature* 132, no. 1 (2013): 139. Accessed September 6, 2020. ATLA Religion Database with ATLASerials, EBSCOhost.

Berman, Joshua. "CTH 133 and the Hittite Provenance of Deuteronomy 13." *Journal of Biblical Literature* 130, no. 1 (Spr 2011): 38. Accessed July 4, 2021. ATLA Religion Database with ATLASerials, EBSCOhost.

Bickerman, Elias Joseph. "Symbolism in the Dura Synagogue." *Harvard Theological Review* 58, no. 1 (Jan 1965): 127. Accessed October 13, 2020. ATLA Religion Database with ATLASerials, EBSCOhost.

Blue, J. Ronald. *Bible Knowledge Commentary: An Exposition of the Scriptures by Dallas Seminary Faculty: New Testament Edition.* Edited by John F. Walvoord and Roy B. Zuck. Colorado Springs: ChariotVictor Publishing, 1983.

Box, Charles. "Bible Commentaries: Charles Box's Commentaries on Selected Books of the Bible: Acts 7." Studylight.org. 2014. https://www.studylight.org/commentaries/box/acts-7.html.

Brettler, Marc, and Amy-Jill Levine. "Isaiah's Suffering Servant: Before and After Christianity." *Interpretation* 73, no. 2 (Apr 2019): 161. Accessed August 31, 2021. ATLA Religion Database with ATLASerials, EBSCOhost.

Brueggemann, Walter. "On Appearing Before the Authorities." *Journal for Preachers* 36, no. 4 (Pentecost 2013): 22-23. Accessed January 24, 2021. ATLA Religion Database with ATLASerials, EBSCOhost.

Brodie, Thomas L. "Towards Unraveling the Rhetorical Imitation of Sources in Acts: 2 Kgs 5 as One Component of Acts 8:9-40." *Biblica* 67, no. 1 (1986): 47. Accessed June 11, 2021. ATLA Religion Database with ATLASerials, EBSCOhost.

Brown, David. "The Acts of the Apostles: Commentary by David Brown: Chapter 8." Blue Letter Bible. Accessed July 16, 2021. https://www.blueletterbible.org/Comm/jfb/Act/Act_008.cfm?a=1026023.

Brown, William P. "The Joy of Lex and the Language of Glory in Psalm 19." *Journal for Preachers* 43, no. 4 (Pentecost 2020): 12-13. Accessed January 20, 2021. ATLA Religion Database with ATLASerials, EBSCOhost.

Burns, J. Lanier. "John 14:1-27: The Comfort of God's Presence." *Bibliotheca sacra* 172, no. 687 (Jul – Sep 2015): 311. Accessed August 17, 2020, ATLA Religion Database with ATLASerials, EBSCOhost.

Carman, Amy Smith. "Ave Maria: Old Testament Allusions in the Magnificat." *Priscilla Papers* 31, no. 2 (Spr 2017): 16. Accessed March 16, 2021. ATLA Religion Database with ATLASerials, EBSCOhost.

Carson, Thomas Scott. "Confessions of an Impotent Potentate: Reading Daniel 4 through the Lens of Ritual Punishment Theory." *Journal for the Study of the Old Testament* 39, no. 1 (Sep 2014): 86. Accessed June 15, 2021. ATLA Religion Database with ATLASerials, EBSCOhost.

Carver, Gary L. "Acts 2:42-47." *Review & Expositor* 87, no. 3 (Sum 1990): 476. Accessed August 25, 2020. ATLA Religion Database with ATLASerials, EBSCOhost.

Chrysostom, John. "Homilies of St. John Chrysostom, Archbishop of Constantinople, on the First Epistle of St. Paul the Apostle. To the Corinthians. – Homily III." Internet Sacred Test Archive. Accessed September 1, 2020. https://www.sacred-texts.com/chr/ecf/112/1120007.htm

Clarke, Adam. "Forerunner Commentary." BIBLETOOLS. Accessed July 16, 2019. https://www.Bibletools.org/index.cfm/fuseaction/Bible.show/sVerseID/27105/eVerseID/27105/RTD/Clarke.

———. "The Adam Clarke Commentary: Chapter 2." StudyLight.org. Accessed September 7, 2020. http://classic.studylight.org/com/acc/view.cgi?book=ac&chapter=002.

Coffman, James Burton. "Bible Commentaries: Coffman Commentaries on the Bible: 2 Peter 3." Studylight.org. Accessed February 28, 2021. https://www.studylight.org/commentaries/eng/bcc/2-peter-3.html

———. "Bible Commentaries: Coffman Commentaries on the Bible: Acts 6." Studylight.org. Accessed September 30, 2020. https://www.studylight.org/commentaries/bcc/acts-6.html.

Coffman, Kristofer. "Powers and Authorities: Preaching Romans 8:35-39." *Word & World* 39, no. 3 (Sum 2019): 275. Accessed August 20, 2020. ATLA Religion Database with ATLASerials, EBSCOhost.

Coleman, Rachel L. "The Lukan Beatitudes (Luke 6.20–26) in the Canonical Choir: A 'Test Case' for John Christopher Thomas' Hermeneutical Proposal." *Journal of Pentecostal Theology* 26, no. 1 (2017): 63. Accessed October 14, 2020. ATLA Religion Database with ATLASerials, EBSCOhost.

Collins, Martin G. "Basic Doctrines: The Laying on of Hands." BIBLETOOLS. Accessed July 20, 2020. https://www.bibletools.org/index.cfm/fuseaction/Library.sr/CT/BS/k/235/Basic-Doctrines-Laying-On-of-Hands.htm.

"Commentaries." BIBLETOOLS. Accessed March 12, 2021. https://www.bibletools.org/index.cfm/fuseaction/Bible.show/sVerseID/23248/eVerseID/23249.

"Commentaries: People's Commentary (NT)." BIBLETOOLS. Accessed May 13, 2021. https://www.bibletools.org/index.cfm/fuseaction/Bible.show/sVerseID/27184/eVerseID/27184/RTD/pcnt.

Coxall, Paul. "Repentance: A Change of Heart, a Change in Direction." UtG: Understanding the Gospel (blog). July 22, 2020. Accessed July

20, 2021. https://understandingthegospel.org/blogs/paul-coxall/repentance-a-change-of-heart-a-change-in-direction/.

Crabbe, Kylie. "Being Found Fighting Against God: Luke's Gamaliel and Josephus on Human Responses to Divine Providence." *Zeitschrift für die neutestamentliche Wissenschaft und die Kunde der älteren Kirche* 106, no. 1 (2015): 32. Accessed April 18, 2020. ATLA Religion Database with ATLASerials, EBSCO host.

Culver, Robert Duncan. "Apostles and the Apostolate in the New Testament." *Bibliotheca sacra* 134, no. 534 (Apr-Jun): 136. Accessed September 8, 2020. ATLA Religion Database with ATLASerials, EBSCOhost.

Dale, Robert D. *Pastoral Leadership.* Nashville: Abingdon Press 1986.

Decock, Paul B. "The Understanding of Isaiah 53:7-8 in Acts 8:32-33." *Neotestamentica* 14 (1981): 111. Accessed September 3, 2021. ATLA Religion Database with ATLASerials, EBSCOhost.

"Definitions: The Meaning of Azotus in the Bible." BIBLETOOLS. Accessed September 17, 2021, https://www.bibletools.org/index.cfm/fuseaction/Def.show/RTD/Easton/ID/379/Azotus.htm.

Downs, Bert E. "The Spiritual Gift of Teaching." *Christian Education Journal* 6, no. 1 (1985): 63. Accessed March 24, 2020. ATLA Religion Database with ATLASerials, EBSCOhost.

Dube, Zorodzai. "The Ethiopian Eunuch in Transit: A Migrant Theoretical Perspective." *Hervormde Teologiese Studies* 69, no. 1 (2013): 2. Accessed July 25, 2021. ATLA Religion Database with ATLASerials, EBSCOhost.

Dunelm, Handley. "The Meaning of Faith of Faith in the Bible." BIBLETOOLS. Accessed September 18, 2020. https://www.bibletools.org/index.cfm/fuseaction/Def.show/RTD/ISBE/ID/3349/Faith.htm.

Eckel, Paul T. "Ephesians 6:10-20." *Interpretation* 45, no. 3 (Jul 1991): 289. Accessed January 20, 2021. ATLA Religion Database with ATLASerials, EBSCOhost.

Elbert, Paul. "Acts 2:38 in Light of the Syntax of Imperative—Future Passive and Imperative—Present Participle Combinations." *The Catholic Biblical Quarterly* 75, no. 1 (Jan 2013): 95. Accessed July 13, 2021. ATLA Religion Database with ATLASerials, EBSCOhost.

"Ellicott's Commentary for English Readers." Bible Hub. Accessed November 29, 2020. https://biblehub.com/commentaries/ellicott/john/13.htm.

———. Bible Hub. Accessed December 29, 2020. https://biblehub.com/commentaries/ellicott/acts/7.htm.

———. Bible Hub. Accessed August 8, 2021. https://biblehub.com/commentaries/ellicott/acts/10.htm.

———. Bible Hub. Accessed August 11, 2021, https://biblehub.com/commentaries/ellicott/acts/8.htm.

———. Bible Hub. Accessed August 29,2021, https://biblehub.com/commentaries/ellicott/isaiah/53.htm.

Everett, Gary H. "Bible Commentaries: Gary H. Everett Study Notes on the Holy Scriptures: Luke 4." StudyLight.org. Accessed July 2, 2021. https://www.studylight.org/commentaries/eng/ghe/luke-4.html#verse-14.

"Exodus 1:21." Bible Hub. Accessed October 12, 2021. https://biblehub.com/exodus/1-21.htm.

"Expositor's Greek Testament." Biblehub.com. Accessed September 29, 2020. https://biblehub.com/commentaries/egt/1_corinthians/1.htm.

Findlay, G.G. *Hastings' Dictionary of the Bible*. Edited by James Hastings. Harrington DE: Delmarva Publications, 2014. Kindle.

Flemming, Donald C. "Bible Commentaries: Bridgeway Bible Commentary: 1 Corinthians 2." StudyLight.org. https://www.studylight.org/commentaries/eng/bbc/1-corinthians-2.html#copyright.

"Forerunner Commentary." BIBLETOOLS. Accessed July 15, 2021. https://www.bibletools.org/index.cfm/fuseaction/Bible.show/sVerseID/27190/eVerseID/27190.

Franklin, Patrick S. "The God Who Sends is The God Who Loves: Mission as Participating in the Ecstatic Love of the Triune God." *Didaskalia* 28, (2017-2018): 75-76. Accessed April 20, 2020. ATLA Religion Database with ATLASerials, EBSCOhost.

Friesen, Abraham. "Acts 10: The Baptism of Cornelius as Interpreted by Thomas Müntzer and Felix Manz." The *Mennonite Quarterly Review* 64, no. 1 (Jan 1990): 7. Accessed July 30, 2021. ATLA Religion Database with ATLASerials, EBSCOhost.

"G80 – adelphos–[Thayer's] Greek Lexicon." Blue Letter Bible. Accessed June 6, 2020. https://www.blueletterBible.org/lang/lexicon/lexicon.cfm?Strongs=G80&t=ESV.

"G816 – atenizō – Outline of Biblical Usage." Blue Letter Bible. Accessed January 19, 2021. https://www.blueletterbible.org/lang/lexicon.cfm?Strongs=G816&t=ESV.

"G907 – baptizō – Outline of Biblical Usage." Blue Letter Bible. Accessed March 11, 2021. https://www.blueletterbible.org/lang/lexicon.cfm?Strongs=G907&t=ESV.

"G907 – baptizō – Thayer's Greek Lexicon." Blue Letter Bible. Accessed March 11, 2021. https://www.blueletterbible.org/lang/lexicon.cfm?Strongs=G907&t=ESV.

"G1112 – gongysmos – Outline of Biblical Usage." Blue Letter Bible. Accessed May 20, 2020. https://www.blueletterBible.org/lang/lexicon/lexicon.cfm?Strongs=G1112&t=ESV.

"G1289–diaspeirō – Root Word (Etymology)." Blue Letter Bible. Accessed March 16, 2021. https://www.blueletterbible.org/lang/lexicon/lexicon.cfm?Strongs=G1289&t=ESV.

"G1577 – ekklēsia – Thayer's Greek Lexicon." Accessed April 28, 2020. https://www.blueletterBible.org/lang/lexicon/lexicon.cfm?Strongs=G1577&t=ESV.

"G2097 – euangelizō – Root Word (Etymology)." Blue Letter Bible. Accessed March 5, 2021. https://www.blueletterbible.org/lang/lexicon/lexicon.cfm?Strongs=G2097&t=KJV.

"G2099 – *euangelistēs* – Outline of Biblical Usage." Blue Letter Bible. Accessed October 6, 2021. https://www.blueletterbible.org/lexicon/g2099/kjv/tr/0-1/.

"G2784 – kēryssō – Concordance Results Using ESV." Blue Letter Bible. Accessed April 28. 2021. https://www.blueletterbible.org/lang/lexicon/lexicon.cfm?Strongs=G2784&t=ESV.

"G2784 – kēryssō – Transliteration." Blue Letter Bible. Accessed April 28, 2021. https://www.blueletterbible.org/lang/lexicon/lexicon.cfm?Strongs=G2784&t=ESV.

"G2962 – kyrios – Strong's Definitions / Concordance Results Using ESV." Blue Letter Bible. Accessed February 3, 2021. https://www.blueletterbible.org/lang/lexicon/lexicon.cfm?page=6&strongs=G2962&t=ESV#lexResults.

"G3140 – martyreō – Thayer's Greek Lexicon." Blue Letter Bible. Accessed June 6, 2020. https://www.blueletterBible.org/lang/lexicon/lexicon.cfm?Strongs=G3140&t=ESV.

"G4198 – poreuō – Tools." Blue Letter Bible. Accessed April 7, 2021. https://www.blueletterbible.org/esv/mat/28/19/t_conc_957019

"H7200 – rā'â – Outline of Biblical Usage." Blue Letter Bible. Accessed September 12, 2021. https://www.blueletterbible.org/lexicon/h7200/esv/wlc/0-1/.

Gaebelein, Arno. "Bible Commentaries: Arno Gaebelein's Annotated Bible: Isaiah 59." StudyLight.org. Accessed August 29, 2021. https://www.studylight.org/commentaries/eng/gab/isaiah-59.html.

Gandi, Herald. "The Resurrection: "According to the Scriptures"?" *The Master's Seminary Blog.* July 31, 2018, https://blog.tms.edu/resurrection-according-to-scriptures.

Geisler, Norman L. *Bible Knowledge Commentary: An Exposition of the Scriptures by Dallas Seminary Faculty: New Testament Edition.*

Edited by John F. Walvoord and Roy B. Zuck. Colorado Springs: Chariot Victor Publishing, 1983.

Gerig, Wesley L. "Walk." Biblestudytools.com. Accessed January 12, 2021. https://www.biblestudytools.com/dictionary/walk/.

Gill, John. *Exposition of the Old and New Testament.* Accessed July 12, 2019. http://www.sacred-texts.com/bib/cmt/gill/act006.htm.

Gombis, Timothy G. "Being the Fullness of God in Christ by the Spirit: Ephesians 5:18 in its Epistolary Setting." *Tyndale Bulletin* 53, no. 2 (2002): 265. Accessed January 10, 2021. ATLA Religion Database with ATLASerials, EBSCOhost.

Goodrick, Edward W. "Let's Put 2 Timothy 3:16 Back in the Bible." *Journal of the Evangelical Theological Society* 25, no. 4 (Dec 1982): 485. Accessed December 9, 2020. ATLA Religion Database with ATLASerials, EBSCOhost.

Gorman, Heather M. "Stone-Campbell Interpretations of the Ethiopian Eunuch (Acts 8:26-40): Observations on the Last 50 Years." *Stone-Campbell Journal* 23, no. 1 (Spr 2020): 13. Accessed September 14, 2021. ATLA Religion Database with ATLASerials, EBSCOhost.

Grierson, Charles T.P. *Hastings Dictionary of the Bible (4 Volumes in One): A Dictionary of the Bible.* Edited by James Hastings, D.D. Harrington, DE: Delmarva Publications. Kindle.

Guy, Samuel. "A Politeuma Worth Pursuing: Philippians 3:20 in Light of Philippi's Sociological Composition." *Stone-Campbell Journal* 22, no. 1 (Spr 2019): 90, 98. Accessed April 23, 2020. ATLA Religion Database with ATLASerials, EBSCO host.

Guzik, David. "Acts 6 – The Appointment of Deacons and the Arrest of Stephen." Enduringword.com, https://enduringword.com/bible-commentary/acts-6/.

———. "Study Guide for Acts 7." Blue Letter Bible. Accessed January 27, 2021. https://www.blueletterbible.org/Comm/guzik_david/StudyGuide2017-Act/Act-7.cfm?a=1025057.

———. "Study Guide for Acts 8." Blue Letter Bible. Accessed July 6, 2021. https://www.blueletterbible.org/Comm/guzik_david/StudyGuide2017-Act/Act-8.cfm?a=1026014.

Habel, Norman C. "Symbolism of Wisdom in Proverbs 1-9." *Interpretation* 26, no. 2 (Apr 1972): 146. Accessed July 25, 2021. ATLA Religion Database with ATLASerials, EBSCOhost.

Hamon, Steven A. "Beyond Self-actualization: Comments on the Life and Death of Stephen the Martyr." *Journal of Psychology & Theology* 5, no. 4 (Fall 1977): 292. Accessed September 18, 2020. ATLA Religion Database with ATLASerials, EBSCOhost.

Hartin, Patrick J. *Paul's Social Network: Brothers and Sisters in Faith: Apollos: Paul's Partner or Rival?* Edited by Bruce J. Malina. Collegeville, Minnesota: Liturgical Press.

Hays, Richard B. *Echoes of Scripture in the Letters of Paul.* New Haven: Yale University Press, 1989.

Hebrew-Aramaic & Greek Dictionary. bible.lockman.org. https://bible.lockman.org/htm_php-c.php?do=show_marg_and_gh&b=44&c=8&v=5

Hegstad, Harald. "A Minority Within the Majority: On the Relation Between the Church as Folk Church and as a Community of Believers." *Studia Theologica* 53, no. 2 (1999): 119-121. Accessed April 6, 2020. ATLA Religion Database with ATLASerials, EBSCOhost.

Heidebrecht, Doug. "Distinction and Function in the Church: Reading Galatians 3:38 in Context." *Direction* 34, no. 2 (Fall 2005): 185. Accessed August 21, 2020. ATLA Religion Database with ATLASerials, EBSCO host.

Henry, Matthew. *Commentary on the Whole Bible by Matthew Henry.* Edited by Rev. Leslie F. Church, Ph.D., F.R.Hist.S. Grand Rapids: Zondervan Publishing House.

Hiebert, D. Edmond. "Following Jesus." *Direction* 10, no. 2 (April 1981): 33. Accessed October 28, 2019. ATLA Religion Database with ATLASerials, EBSCOhost.

Higgins, Ryan S. "The Good, the God, and the Ugly: The Role of the Beloved Monster in the Ancient Near East and the Hebrew Bible." *Interpretation* 74, no. 2 (Apr 2020): 135. Accessed November 27, 2020. ATLA Religion Database with ATLASerials, EBSCOhost.

Hodges, Zane C. *Bible Knowledge Commentary: An Exposition of the Scriptures by Dallas Seminary Faculty: New Testament Edition.* Edited by John F. Walvoord and Roy B. Zuck. Colorado Springs: ChariotVictor Publishing, 1983.

Holmgren, Fredrick Carlson. "The Pharisee and the Tax Collector: Luke 18:9-14 and Deuteronomy 26:1-15." *Interpretation* 48, no. 3 (Jul 1994): 253. Accessed June 8, 2021. ATLA Religion Database with ATLASerials, EBSCOhost.

Horton, Howard. "The Gates of Hades Shall Not Prevail Against It." *Restoration Quarterly* 5, no. 1 (1961): 4. Accessed August 26, 2020. ATLA Religion Database with ATLASerials, EBSCOhost.

Huizenga, Annette Bourland. "Paul as Pastor in 1 Timothy, 2 Timothy, and Titus." *The Bible Today* 51, no. 5 (Sep-Oct 2013): 299. Accessed August 27, 2020. ATLA Religion Database with ATLASerials, EBSCOhost.

Hunn, Debbie. "Pleasing God or Pleasing People? Defending the Gospel in Galatians 1-2." *Biblica* 91, no.1 (2010): 34-39. Accessed June 22, 2020. ATLA Religion Database with ATLASerials, EBSCOhost.

Hunt, Joseph I. "Translating Psalm 29: Towards a Commentary on the Psalms of the 1979 Book of Common Prayer." *Anglican Theological Review* 67, no. 3 (Jul 1985): 222. Accessed November 11, 2020. ATLA Religion Database with ATLASerials, EBSCOhost.

Jabini, Franklin S. "Preaching Christ in a Pluralistic World: The Message and Method of the Mission to Samaria in Acts 8." *Conspectus* 9 (Mar 2010): 59. Accessed May 11, 2021. ATLA Religion Database with ATLASerials, EBSCOhost.

Jacobs, Joseph, and Isaac Broyde'. "Tax-Gatherers," JewishEncyclopedia.com, http://www.jewishencyclopedia.com/articles/14273-tax-gatherers.

Johnson, Barton W. "Bible Commentaries: People's New Testament: Acts 6." Studylight.org. Accessed October 16, 2020. https://www.studylight.org/commentaries/pnt/acts-6.html.

Joubert, Callie, and Nick Maartens. "Hearing God's Voice: Evaluating Some Popular Teachings on the Subject." *Conspectus* 25, (25 March 2018): 52. Accessed March 25, 2020. ATLA Religion Database with ATLASerials, EBSCOhost.

Joubert, Stephen. "Behind the Mask of Rhetoric: 2 Corinthians 8 and the Intra-textual Relation Between Paul and the Corinthians." *Neotestamentica* 26, no. 1 (1992): 107. Accessed September 21, 2020. ATLA Religion Database with ATLASerials, EBSCOhost.

Juel, Donald H. "Hearing Peter's Speech in Acts 3: Meaning and Truth in Interpretation." *Word & Word* 12, no. 1 (Wint 1992): 45. Accessed May 13, 2021. ATLA Religion Database with ATLASerials, EBSCOhost.

Keefer, Kyle A. "Philip, Samaria, and God's Plan." America: The Jesuit Review. Accessed June 28, 2021. https://www.americamagazine.org/content/good-word/philip-samaria-and-gods-plan.

Keener, Craig S. *The IVP Bible Background Commentary New Testament*. Downers Grove: Intervarsity Press, 1993.

Kim, Ju-Won. "Explicit Quotations from Genesis Within the Context of Stephen's Speech in Acts." *Neotestamentica* 41, no. 2 (2007): 355. Accessed November 24, 2020. ATLA Religion Database with ATLASerials, EBSCOhost.

Kirby, Jeffery. "The Depth of the Beatitudes: Christ Spells Out the Path to Holiness, Happiness in Matthew 5." *The Priest* 75, no. 4 (Apr 2019): 43. Accessed August 6, 2021. ATLA Religion Database with ATLASerials, EBSCOhost.

Kirchhevel, Gordon D. "The Children of God and the Glory that John 1:14 Saw." *Bulletin of Biblical Research* 6, (1996): 89. Accessed October 5, 2020. ATLA Religion Database with ATLASerials, EBSCOhost.

Kislev, Itamar. "Joshua (and Caleb) in the Priestly Spies Story and Joshua's Initial Appearance in the Priestly Source: A Contribution to an Assessment of the Pentateuchal Priestly Material." *Journal of Biblical Literature* 136, no. 1 (2017): 48. Accessed July 8, 2020. ATLA Religion Database with ATLASerials, EBSCOhost.

Klaiber, Walter. "The Great Commission of Matthew 28:16-20." *American Baptist Quarterly* 37, no.2 (Sum 2018): 110. Accessed February 10, 2021. ATLA Religion Database with ATLASerials, EBSCOhost.

Kleiman, Kevin. "The Suffering of Jesus." Cities Church. Last modified July 22, 2018. https://www.citieschurch.com/sermons/the-suffering-of-jesus.

Klein, William W., Craig L. Blomberg, and Robert L. Hubbard, Jr. *Introduction to Biblical Interpretation*, rev. ed. Nashville: Thomas Nelson Publishers, 2004.

Klooster, Anton ten. "Aquinas on the Fruits of the Holy Spirit as the Delight of the Christian Life," *Journal of Moral Theology* 8, (Spr 2019): 84. Accessed May 14, 2021. ATLA Religion Database with ATLASerials, EBSCOhost.

Kohler, Kaufmann. "Heaven." JewishEncyclopedia.com. Accessed April 18, 2020. http://www.jewishencyclopedia.com/articles/7440-heaven.

———. "Kingdom of God ("Malkuta de-Adonai")." JewishEncyclopedia.com. Accessed April 18, 2020, http://www.jewishencyclopedia.com/articles/9328-kingdom-of-god.

Lange, John Peter. "Lange Commentary on the Holy Scriptures." Biblehub.com. Accessed February 21, 2021. https://biblehub.com/commentaries/lange/matthew/13.htm.

Lanker, Jason. "The Family of Faith: The Place of Natural Mentoring in the Church's Christian Formation of Adolescents." *Christian*

Education Journal 7, no. 2 (Fall 2010): 268. Accessed August 25, 2020. ATLA Religion Database with ATLASerials, EBSCOhost.

Litfin, A. Duane. *Bible Knowledge Commentary: An Exposition of the Scriptures by Dallas Seminary Faculty: Old Testament.* Edited by John F. Walvoord and Roy B. Zuck. N.P.: SP Publications, 1985.

Lockyer, Herbert Sr., ed., *Nelson's Illustrated Bible Dictionary* (Nashville: Thomas Nelson Publishers, 1986), 942.

Lowery, David K. *Bible Knowledge Commentary: An Exposition of the Scriptures by Dallas Seminary Faculty: New Testament Edition.* Edited by John F. Walvoord and Roy B. Zuck. Colorado Springs: ChariotVictor Publishing, 1983.

Lumby, J.R., ed. *The Acts of the Apostles.* The University Press, 1888. Google Play.

MacArthur, John. *The MacArthur Study Bible English Standard Version.* Wheaton, Illinois: Crossway, 2010.

Macaskill, Grant. "Union(s) with Christ: Colossians 1:15-20." *Ex auditu* 33, (2017): 99. Accessed April 27, 2020. ATLA Religion Database with ATLASerials, EBSCO host.

Mackie, Scott D. "Visually Oriented Rhetoric and Visionary Experience in Hebrews 12:1-4." *The Catholic Biblical Quarterly* 79, no. 3 (Jul 2017): 492. Accessed August 11, 2021. ATLA Religion Database with ATLASerials, EBSCOhost.

Malone, Andrew S. "Distinguishing the Angel of the Lord." *Bulletin for Biblical Research* 21, no. 3 (2011): 301. Accessed July 25, 2021. ATLA Religion Database with ATLASerials, EBSCOhost.

Massey, Denise M. "A Word About: Praying When You are Afraid (Phil 4:6-7)." *Review & Expositor* 115, no. 2 (2018): 268. Accessed October 19, 2020. ATLA Religion Database with ATLASerials, EBSCOhost.

Mayes, Benjamin T G. "The Useful Application of Scripture in Lutheran Orthodoxy: An Aid to Contemporary Preaching and Exegesis." *Concordia Theology Quarterly* 83, no. 1-2 (Jan-Apr 2019): 128.

Accessed November 23, 2020. ATLA Religion Database with ATLASerials, EBSCOhost.

McBride, S. Dean. "The Yoke of the Kingdom: An Exposition of Deuteronomy 6:4-5." *Interpretation* 27, no. 3 (Jul 1973): 285. Accessed April 22, 2020. ATLA Religion Database with ATLASerials, EBSCOhost.

McGarvey, J. W. "Bible Commentaries: McGarvey's Original Commentary on Acts: Acts 6." Studylight.org. Accessed September 30, 2020. https://www.studylight.org/commentaries/oca/acts-6.html.

McIntyre, Luther B. Jr. "Baptism and Forgiveness in Acts 2:38." *Bibliotheca sacra* 153, no. 609 (Jan-Mar 1996): 57. Accessed July 14, 2021. ATLA Religion Database with ATLASerials, EBSCOhost.

Melbourne, Bertram L. "Acts 1:8 Re-Examined: Is Acts 8 Its Fulfillment?" *The Journal of Religious Thought* 57, no. 2 (January 1, 2005): 8. Accessed March 19, 2021. ATLA Religion Database with ATLASerials, EBSCOhost.

Merriam-Webster. *Webster's Ninth New Collegiate College Dictionary*. Springfield, MA: Merriam-Webster, Inc., 1985.

Meyer, Dale A. "Why Go to Church Every Sunday? Three Reasons from 1 Peter." *Concordia Journal* 45, no. 1 (Wint 2019): 9. Accessed October 27, 2020. ATLA Religion Database with ATLASerials, EBSCOhost.

Millar, Fergus. "Inscriptions, Synagogues and Rabbis in Late Antique Palestine." *Journal for the Study of Judaism* 42, no. 2 (2011): 272. Accessed October 10, 2020. ATLA Religion Database with ATLASerials, EBSCOhost.

Miller, Amanda C. "Paul's Social Network in Colossians: Friends and Coworkers in the Lycus Valley." *Review & Expositor* 116, no. 4 (Nov 2019): 437. Accessed January 19, 2021. ATLA Religion Database with ATLASerials, EBSCOhost.

Minnicks, Margaret. "Singleness: What the Bible Says About Being Single." PairedLife. Accessed October 13, 2021. https://pairedlife.com/single-life/Singleness-What-the-Bible-Says-about-Being-Single.

Mitternacht, Dieter. "Knowledge-making and Myth-making in John 6: A Narrative-Psychological Reading." *Svensk Exegetisk Arsbok* 72, (2007): 59. Accessed October 14, 2020. ATLA Religion Database with ATLASerials, EBSCOhost.

Mowczko, Marg. "Living as Lights in the World – Philippians 2:12-18." Marg Mowczko: Exploring the Biblical Theology of Christian Egalitarianism. Accessed June 18, 2021. https://margmowczko.com/philippians-2_12-18/.

Murphy, Bryan. "The Unalterable Word." *The Master's Seminary Journal* 26, no. 2 (Fall 2015): 171. Accessed September 4, 2020. ATLA Religion Database with ATLASerials, EBSCOhost.

Nash, Charles Harris. "Stephen, the Model Layman: The Unique, Transcendent Image of Jesus in Life and Death, 'Filled with all the Fulness of God.' Acts 6-7." *Review & Expositor* 23, no. 4 (Oct 1926): 452. Accessed September 15, 2020. ATLA Religion Database with ATLASerials, EBSCOhost.

Nasuti, Harry P. "Repentance and Transformation: The Role of the Spirit in Psalm 51." *The Bible Today* 57, no. 4 (Jul-Aug 2019): 215. Accessed March 23, 2020. ATLA Religion Database with ATLASerials, EBSCOhost.

Nation, Steven. "Martyr in Every Sense of the Word: Learning from the Life and Death of Stephen, the First Known Martyr." *Churchman* 125, no. 2 (Sum 2011): 176. Accessed January 10, 2021. ATLA Religion Database with ATLASerials, EBSCOhost.

Neyrey, Jerome H. S.J., and Richard L Rohrbaugh. "He Must Increase, I Must Decrease (John 3:30): A Cultural and Social Interpretation." *The Catholic Biblical Quarterly* 63, no. 3 (Jul 2001): 465. Accessed July 16, 2021. ATLA Religion Database with ATLASerials, EBSCOhost.

Nullens, Patrick. "Theologia Caritatis and the Moral Authority of Scripture: Approaching 2 Timothy 3:16-17 with a Hermeneutic of

Love." *European Journal of Theology* 22, no. 1 (2013): 45. Accessed March 24, 2020. ATLA Religion Database with ATLASerials, EBSCOhost.

Nyk, Piotr. "You are Witnesses of These Things! (Luke 24:48): The Concept of Testimony in the Gospel of Luke." *Verbum Vitae* 27, (2015): 121. Accessed December 23, 2020. ATLA Religion Database with ATLASerials, EBSCOhost.

O'Loughlin, Thomas. "The Diversifying Spirit: The Gift of Pentecost." *The Pastoral Review* 11, no. 3 (May-Jun 2015): 4, 7. Accessed September 2, 2020. ATLA Religion Database with ATLASerials, EBSCOhost.

O'Toole, Peter F. "What Role Does Jesus' Saying in Acts 20,35 Play in Paul's Address to the Ephesian Elders?" *Biblica* 75, no. 3 (1994): 335-336. Accessed August 28, 2020. ATLA Religion Database with ATLASerials, EBSCOhost.

Ortlund, Dane C. "What Does it Mean to Fall Short of the Glory of God? Romans 3:23 in Biblical-Theological Perspective." *The Westminster Theological Journal* 80. Accessed June 18, 2021. ATLA Religion Database with ATLASerials, EBSCOhost.

Overland, Paul. "Did the Sage Draw from the Shema? A Study of Proverbs 3:1-2." *The Catholic Biblical Quarterly* 62, no. 3 (Jul 2000): 424-440. Accessed May 24, 2020. ATLA Religion Database with ATLASerials, EBSCOhost.

Patella, Michael. "Do Not Hold This Sin Against Them – The Martyrdom of Stephen (Acts 7)." *The Bible Today* 55, no. 3 (May-Jun 2017): 198-199. Accessed November 18, 2020. ATLA Religion Database with ATLASerials, EBSCOhost.

Payton, James R. Jr. "On Unity and Truth: Martin Bucer's Sermon on John 17." *Calvin Theological Journal* 27, no. 1 (Apr 1992): 34. Accessed August 27, 2020. ATLA Religion Database with ATLASerials, EBSCOhost.

Pao, David W. "Waiters or Preachers: Acts 6:1-7 and the Lukan Table Fellowship Motif." *Journal of Biblical Literature* 130, no. 1 (2011):

127-128. Accessed July 15, 2019. ATLA Religion Database with ATLASerials, EBSCOhost.

Paul, Kolawole Olumafemi. "The Great Commission Mandate of the Church in Matthew 28:18-20." *Word & World* 40, no. 4 (Fall 2020): 424. Accessed February 17, 2021. ATLA Religion Database with ATLASerials, EBSCOhost.

Phanon, Yuri. "The Work of the Holy Spirit in the Conception, Baptism and Temptation of Christ: Implications for the Pentecostal Christian 1." *Asian Journal of Pentecostal Studies* 20, no. 1 (Feb 2017): 37. Accessed July 9, 2021. ATLA Religion Database with ATLASerials, EBSCOhost.

"Philip's Journeys." The Bible Journey. Accessed September 17, 2021. https://www.thebiblejourney.org/biblejourney1/7-journeys-of-jesuss-followers/philips-journeys/.

Piper, John. "How to Receive the Word of Man as the Word of God." desiringGod. Accessed July 6, 2021. https://www.desiringgod.org/messages/how-to-receive-the-word-of-man-as-the-word-of-god.

Polaski, Donald C. "Mene, Mene, Tekel, Parsin: Writing and Resistance in Daniel 5 and 6." *Journal of Biblical Literature* 123, no. 4 (Wint 2004): 656. Accessed September 16, 2020. ATLA Religion Database with ATLASerials, EBSCOhost.

Poole, Matthew. "Matthew Poole's Commentary." Biblehub.com. Accessed April 15, 2020. https://Biblehub.com/commentaries/poole/acts/5.htm.

Pritchett, Johnathan. "New Testament Use of the Old Testament." Lecture, Trinity College of the Bible and Theological Seminary, Evansville, IN.

Procházková, Ivana. "The Torah Within the Heart, In the Feet, and on the Tongue: Law and Freedom in Psalm 119 from the Perspective of Cognitive Linguistics." *Communio viatorum* 54, no. 1 (2012): 21. Accessed August 22, 2021. ATLA Religion Database with ATLASerials, EBSCOhost.

Prothro, James B. "Distance, Tolerance, and Honor: Six Theses on Romans 13:1-7." *Concordia Journal* 42, no. 4 (Fall 2016): 294. Accessed October 30, 2020. ATLA Religion Database with ATLASerials, EBSCOhost.

"Proverbs 14:15." LetGodbeTrue.com. Accessed July 5, 2021. https://letgodbetrue.com/proverbs/index/chapter-14/proverbs-14-15/.

"Pulpit Commentary." Bible Hub. Accessed August 19, 2020. https://biblehub.com/commentaries/pulpit/acts/2.htm.

———. Bible Hub. Accessed September 6, 2020. https://biblehub.com/commentaries/pulpit/1_corinthians/12.htm.

———. Bible Hub. Accessed December 22, 2020. https://biblehub.com/commentaries/pulpit/luke/21.htm.

———. Bible Hub. Accessed April 6, 2021. https://biblehub.com/commentaries/pulpit/matthew/10.htm.

———. Bible Hub. Accessed August 3, 2021. https://biblehub.com/commentaries/pulpit/proverbs/18.htm.

———. Bible Hub. Accessed August 13, 2021. https://biblehub.com/commentaries/pulpit/1_corinthians/14.htm.

———. Bible Hub. Accessed September 8, 2021. https://biblehub.com/commentaries/pulpit/isaiah/53.htm.

Raymer, Roger M. *Bible Knowledge Commentary: An Exposition of the Scriptures by Dallas Seminary Faculty: New Testament Edition.* Edited by John F. Walvoord and Roy B. Zuck. Colorado Springs: ChariotVictor Publishing, 1983.

Reardon, Timothy W. "'Hanging on a Tree': Deuteronomy 21.22-13 and the Rhetoric of Jesus' Crucifixion in Acts 5.12-42." *Journal for the Study of the New Testament* 37, no. 4 (Jun 2015): 423. Accessed September 29, 2020. ATLA Religion Database with ATLASerials, EBSCOhost.

Reid, John O. "What the Bible Says About Continuing in the Faith." BIBLETOOLS. Accessed September 16, 2020. https://www.

Bibliography

bibletools.org/index.cfm/fuseaction/topical.show/RTD/cgg/ID/8552/Continuing-in-Faith.htm.

Renée, Leesa. "The Jethro Principle: The 3 Things You Can Do to Become a Better Leader in Your Ministry or Business." LEESA RENÉE: Exploring Bias One Question at a Time. Accessed July 19, 2021. ATLA Religion Database with ATLASerials, EBSCOhost.

Richard, Earl J. "The Polemical Character of the Joseph Episode in Acts 7." *Journal of Biblical Literature* 98, no. 2 (Jun 1979): 257. Accessed November 18, 2020. ATLA Religion Database with ATLASerials, EBSCOhost.

Ritenbaugh, John W. "Commentaries: Forerunner Commentary – Acts 7:24-25." BIBLETOOLS. Accessed October 8, 2021. https://www.bibletools.org/index.cfm/fuseaction/Bible.show/sVerseID/27142/eVerseID/27142.

———. "Commentaries: Forerunner Commentary: 2 Corinthians 10:3-5." BIBLETOOLS. Accessed July 15, 2021. https://www.bibletools.org/index.cfm/fuseaction/Bible.show/sVerseID/28977/eVerseID/28977/version/gnb.

———. "Commentaries: Forerunner Commentary – Colossians 1:9-11." BIBLETOOLS. Accessed June 18, 2020. https://www.bibletools.org/index.cfm/fuseaction/Bible.show/sVerseID/29475/eVerseID/29475.

Ritenbaugh, Richard T. "What the Bible Says About Diviner." BIBLETOOLS. Accessed June 11, 2021. https://www.bibletools.org/index.cfm/fuseaction/Topical.show/RTD/CGG/ID/12956/Diviner.htm.

———. "Commentaries: Forerunner Commentary – 1 Corinthians 15:33." BIBLETOOLS. Accessed August 25, 2020. https://www.bibletools.org/index.cfm/fuseaction/bible.show/sVerseID/28752/eVerseID/28752.

Roark, C. Mack. "Interpreting Ephesians 4-6: God's People in a Walk Worthy of His Calling." *Southwestern Journal of Theology* 39, no.1 (Fall 1996): 37. Accessed July 26, 2020. ATLA Religion Database with ATLASerials, EBSCOhost.

Robertson, Cleotha A. "Psalm 1: A Guide for Spiritual Formation." *The Living Pulpit (Online)* 27, no. 1 (Spr 2018): 4. Accessed May 28, 2021. ATLA Religion Database with ATLASerials, EBSCOhost.

Sadaphal, C. H. "Connectivity: Acts 17." *The Living Pulpit (Online)* 24, no. 4 (Winter 2015): 14-16. Accessed March 26, 2020. ATLA Religion Database with ATLASerials, EBSCOhost.

Schenck, Kenneth L. "A Celebration of the Enthroned Son: The Catena of Hebrews 1." *Journal of Biblical Literature* 120, no. 3 (Fall 2001): 472. Accessed January 20, 2021. ATLA Religion Database with ATLASerials, EBSCOhost.

Schenk, Kara L. "Temple, Community, and Sacred Narrative in the Dura-Europos Synagogue." *AJS Review* 34, no. 2 (Nov 2010): 198. Accessed October 13, 2020. ATLA Religion Database with ATLASerials, EBSCOhost.

Schrock, David. "The Arm of the Lord: From Moses to Isaiah to Christ." VIA EMMAUS. Published December 13, 2017. https://davidschrock.com/2017/12/13/the-arm-of-the-lord-from-moses-to-isaiah-to-christ/.

Scott, J. Julius Jr., "Stephen's Speech: A Possible Model for Luke's Historical Method." *Journal of the Evangelical Theological Society* 17, no. 2 (Spr 1974): 93. Accessed November 18, 2020. ATLA Religion Database with ATLASerials, EBSCOhost.

Seal, David. "The Lord's Prayer Prayed." *Restoration Quarterly* 61, no. 2 (2019): 79-80. Accessed November 12, 2020. ATLA Religion Database with ATLASerials, EBSCOhost.

Searles, Matt. "These Things I Have Said to You: An Investigation of How Purpose Clauses Govern the Interpretation of John 14-16." *Journal of the Evangelical Theological Society* 60, no. 3, (Sep 2017): 515-516. Accessed March 29, 2020. ATLA Religion Database with ATLASerials, EBSCOhost.

Shenk, Calvin E. "God's Intention for Humankind: The Promise of Community: Bible Study on Genesis 12." *Mission Studies* 5, no. 2 (1998): 15. Accessed April 27, 2021. ATLA Religion Database with ATLASerials, EBSCOhost.

Shiell, William D. "'I Will Give You a Mouth and Wisdom'; Prudent Speech in Luke 21:15." *Review & Expositor* 112, no. 4 (Nov 2015): 609. Accessed October 13, 2020. ATLA Religion Database with ATLASerials, EBSCOhost.

Simeon, Charles. "Bible Commentaries: Charles Simeon's Horae Homileticae: Acts 8." StudyLight.org. Accessed April 28, 2021. https://www.studylight.org/commentaries/eng/shh/acts-8.html#verse-5.

Slick, Matt. "Acts 6:1-7 Building the Church of Disciples." CARM: Christian Apologetics & Research Ministry. Accessed August 25, 2020. https://carm.org/sermon-acts-6-1-7-building-church-disciples.

Smillie, Gene R. "'Ο λογοος του θεου' in Hebrews 4:12-13." *Novum Testamentum* 46, no. 4 (2004): p 338, 341. Accessed March 28, 2020. ATLA Religion Database with ATLASerials, EBSCOhost.

Smith, Chuck. "Chuck Smith: Study Guide for Acts." Blue Letter Bible. Accessed July 23, 2021. https://www.blueletterbible.org/Comm/smith_chuck/StudyGuides_Acts/Acts.cfm?a=1026026.

Spencer, F. Scott. "'Follow Me: The Imperious Call of Jesus in the Synoptic Gospels." *Interpretation* 59, no. 2 (April 2005): 142-153. Accessed October 24, 2019. ATLA Religion Database with ATLASerials, EBSCOhost.

"Spiritual Maturity." Grace Covenant Church. Accessed July 2, 2021. https://gracegi.org/sermons/spiritual-maturity-1-corinthians-31-9/.

Spurgeon, Charles Haddon. "Household Salvation." The Spurgeon Center for Biblical Preaching at Midwestern Seminary. Accessed October 20, 2021. https://www.spurgeon.org/resource-library/sermons/household-salvation/#flipbook/.

Stanley, Charles F. "9 Characteristics of a Follower of Jesus: Committing Ourselves to Christ." In Touch Ministries. March 26, 2018. https://www.intouch.org/Read/Blog/9-characteristics-of-a-follower-of-jesus.

Stevens, Gerald L. "Luke 15: Parables of God's Search for Sinners." *The Theological Educator* 56, (Fall 1997): 75. Accessed July 30, 2021. ATLA Religion Database with ATLASerials, EBSCOhost.

Stewart, Hannah R. "Self-emptying and Sacrifice: A Feminist Critique of Kenosis in Philippians 2." *Colloquium* 44, no. 1 (May 2012): 108. Accessed September 5, 2021. ATLA Religion Database with ATLASerials, EBSCOhost.

Stirling, Mark. "Transformed Walking and Missional Temple Building: Discipleship in Ephesians." *Presbyterion* 45, no. 2 (Fall 2019): 86, 92. Accessed September 7, 2020. ATLA Religion Database with ATLASerials, EBSCOhost.

Strickland, Michael. "The (In)Significance of The Baptizer in the Early Church: The Importance of Baptism and Unimportance of the One who Baptized." *Journal of the Evangelical Theological Society* 61, no. 2 (Jun 2018): 355-366. Accessed June 23, 2021. ATLA Religion Database with ATLASerials, EBSCOhost.

Strong, Augustus Hopkins. "The Holy Spirit: The One and Only Power in Missions." *The Journal of the Evangelical Homiletics Society* 7, no. 2 (Sep 2007): 78. Accessed February 26, 2021. ATLA Religion Database with ATLASerials, EBSCOhost.

Strong, James. "A Concise Dictionary of the Words in The Greek Testament; with their Renderings in the Authorized English Version." In *The New Strong's Exhaustive Concordance of the Bible*. Nashville: Thomas Nelson Publishers, 1990

Sunukjian, Donald R. *Bible Knowledge Commentary: An Exposition of the Scriptures by Dallas Seminary Faculty: Old Testament*. Edited by John F. Walvoord and Roy B. Zuck. SP Publications, 1985.

Swindoll, Pastor Chuck. "Priorities." Insight for Today: A Daily Devotional by Pastor Chuck Swindoll. The Bible-Teaching Ministry of Pastor Chuck Swindoll. Accessed May 23, 2020. https://www.insight.org/resources/daily-devotional/individual/priorities.

Syreeni, Kari. "Partial Weaning: Approaching the Psychological Enigma of John 13-17." *Svensk Exegetisk Arsbok* 72, (2007): 183. Accessed

January 29, 2021. ATLA Religion Database with ATLASerials, EBSCOhost.

The Jewish Publication Society of America. *The Holy Scriptures According to the Masoretic Text; A New Translation.* Chicago: The Lakeside Press, 1917.

"The Shema." My Jewish Learning. Accessed May 24, 2020. https://www.myjewishlearning.com/article/the-shema.

Thiessen, Jim Loepp. "What's Stopping You? Philip and the Ethiopian Eunuch (Acts 8:25-39)." *Vision (Winnipeg, Man)* 4, no. 2 (Fall 2003): 54. Accessed July 25, 2021. ATLA Religion Database with ATLASerials, EBSCOhost.

Thompson, Robin G. "Diaspora Jewish Freedmen: Stephen's Deadly Opponents." *Bibliotheca sacra* 173, no. 690 (Apr – Jun 2016): 166. Accessed October 28, 2020. ATLA Religion Database with ATLASerials, EBSCOhost.

Toussaint, Stanley D. *Bible Knowledge Commentary: An Exposition of the Scriptures by Dallas Seminary Faculty: New Testament Edition.* Edited by John F. Walvoord and Roy B. Zuck. Colorado Springs: ChariotVictor Publishing, 1983.

Towner, W. Sibley. "Hermeneutical Systems of Hillel and the Tannaim: A Fresh Look." *Hebrew Union College Annual* 53, (1982): 18. Accessed July 21, 2020. ATLA Religion Database with ATLASerials, EBSCOhost.

Turner, Max. "Interpreting the Samaritans of Acts 8: The Waterloo of Pentecostal Soteriology and Pneumatology?" *Pneuma* 23, no. 2 (Fall 2001): 272. Accessed June 16, 2021. ATLA Religion Database with ATLASerials, EBSCOhost.

Vieira, Celiane. "Isaiah 42: The Mission of the Servant." *Missio apostolica* 22, no. 1 (May 2014): 131, 133. Accessed November 25, 2020. ATLA Religion Database with ATLASerials, EBSCOhost.

Viljoen, Francois P. "Righteousness and Identity Formation in the Sermon on the Mount." *Hervormde Teologiese Studies* 69, no. 1

(2013): 8-9. Accessed May 23, 2020. ATLA Religion Database with ATLASerials, EBSCOhost.

Vine, W.E. *Vine's Expository Dictionary of Old & New Testament Words*. Nashville: Thomas Nelson Publishers, 1997.

Waltke, Bruce. "Friends and Friendship in the Book of **Proverbs**: An Exposition of **Proverbs** 27:1-22." *Crux* 38, no. 3 (Sep 2002): 36. Accessed August 10, 2020. ATLA Religion Database with ATLASerials, EBSCOhost.

Wegener, Mark I. "The Rhetorical Strategy of 1 Corinthians 15." *Currents in Theology and Mission* 31, no. 6 (Dec 2004): 439. Accessed April 29, 2021. ATLA Religion Database with ATLASerials, EBSCOhost.

Wenkel, David H. "The Gnashing of Teeth of Jesus' Opponents." *Bibliotheca sacra* 175, no. 697 (Jan–Mar 2018): 83. Accessed December 23, 2020. ATLA Religion Database with ATLASerials, EBSCOhost.

"What Does 1 Timothy 5:17 Mean?" BibleRef.com. Accessed July 1, 2021. https://www.bibleref.com/1-Timothy/5/1-Timothy-5-17.html#commentary.

"What Does It Mean that God Draws Us to Salvation?" Got Questions: Your Questions: Biblical Answers. Got Questions Ministries. Last updated April 26, 2021. https://www.gotquestions.org/drawn-salvation.html.

"What Does It Mean to "Run the Race Set Before Us" (Hebrews 12:1)?" Got Questions: Your Questions: Biblical Answers, Got Questions Ministries. Last updated April 26, 2021. https://www.gotquestions.org/run-the-race-set-before-us.html.

White, Aaron W. "The Apostolic Preaching of the Lord Jesus: Seeing the Speeches in Acts as a Coherent Series of Sermons." *Presbyterion* 44, no. 2 (Fall 2018): 42. Accessed November 11, 2020. ATLA Religion Database with ATLASerials, EBSCOhost.

White, Devin. "Confronting Oracular Contradiction in Acts 21:1-14." *Novum Testamentum* 58, no. 1 (2016): 34. Accessed October 10, 2021. ATLA Religion Database with ATLASerials, EBSCOhost.

White, Stephen L. "Angel of the Lord: Messenger or Euphemism?" *Tyndale Bulletin* 50, no. 2 (1999): 302. Accessed August 4, 2021. ATLA Religion Database with ATLASerials, EBSCOhost.

"Who was Saul of Tarsus in the Bible?" CompellingTruth. Accessed October 15, 2021. https://www.compellingtruth.org/Saul-of-Tarsus.html.

Wilson, Jennie Bain. "Hold to God's Unchanging Hand." Hymnary.org. Accessed July 23, 2021. https://hymnary.org/text/time_is_filled_with_swift_transition.

Witherington III, Ben. *New Testament Rhetoric: An Introductory Guide to the Art of Persuasion in and of the New Testament*. Eugene, OR: Cascade Books, 2009.

Wolff, Celia I. "Sharing the Gospel as Witness to Jesus: Acts 1:1-11." *Word & World* 39, no. 4 (Fall 2019): 374. Accessed February 21, 2021. ATLA Religion Database with ATLASerials, EBSCOhost.

Woods, Len. *Understanding the Holy Spirit Made Easy*. Peabody, MA: Rose Publishing, LLC, 2018.

Wright, N. T. *The Resurrection Son of God: Christian Origins and the Question of God, Volume 3*. London: Fortress Press, 2003.

Yoder, Christine Roy. "On the Threshold of Kingship: A Study of Agur (Proverbs 30)." *Interpretation* 63, no. 3, (Jul 2009): 261. Accessed September 4, 2020. ATLA Religion Database with ATLASerials, EBSCOhost.